FEAR LESS
FOR LIFE

FEAR LESS
FOR LIFE

BREAK FREE TO LIVING
WITH HOPE AND CONFIDENCE

STEPHEN ARTERBURN

PAUL MEIER

ROBERT L. WISE

THOMAS NELSON PUBLISHERS®
Nashville

A Division of Thomas Nelson, Inc.
www.ThomasNelson.com

Unless otherwise noted, Scripture quotations are from the NEW AMERICAN STANDARD BIBLE®. Copyright © The Lockman Foundation 1960, 1962, 1963, 1968, 1971, 1972, 1973, 1975, 1977. Used by permission.

Scripture quotations noted NKJV are from THE NEW KING JAMES VERSION. Copyright © 1979, 1980, 1982, Thomas Nelson, Inc., Publishers.

Scripture quotations noted NLT are from the *Holy Bible,* New Living Translation, Copyright © 1996. Used by permission of Tyndale House Publishers, Inc., Wheaton, Illinois 60189. All rights reserved.

Scripture quotations noted NIV are from the HOLY BIBLE: NEW INTERNATIONAL VERSION®. Copyright © 1973, 1978, 1984 by International Bible Society. Used by permission of Zondervan Publishing House. All rights reserved.

THE NEW ENGLISH BIBLE. Copyright © 1961, 1970 by the Delegates of the Oxford University Press and the Syndics of the Cambridge University Press. Reprinted by permission.

Library of Congress Cataloging-in-Publication Data Available

Arterburn, Stephen, 1953-
  Fear less for life : break free to living with hope and confidence /Stephen Arterburn, Paul Meier, Robert L. Wise.
      p. cm.
  Includes bibliographical references.
  Contents: pt. 1: Don't even go there-identifying the problem.—1. A path beyond fear—2. Taking a peek in your dark attic—3. Things that go bump in the night—4. Stumbling block or stepping stone?—pt. 2: Turning crisis into confidence-discovering answers—5. The launching pad—6. Getting to the root—7. Trouble in your backyard—8. Not-so-fascinating phobias—9. Stop the attack—10. Nothing like a good night's sleep—11. Fear and food—12. Power from a pill—pt. 3: Nothing to fear . . . but fear itself-building for the future—13. The divine point of view—14. The view from the grave—15. Self-control to the rescue—16. Turning points toward power—17. The greatest of these-love.
  ISBN 0-7852-7803-6
  1. Fear—Religious aspects—Christianity. 2. Fear. 3. Psychoanalysis. I. Meier, Paul D. II. Wise, Robert L. III. Title.
BV4908.5 .A78 2002
248.8'6—dc21

                                                                2002012760

Printed in the United States of America

02 03 04 05 06 BVG 5 4 3 2 1

CONTENTS

CONTENTS

PART 1

Don't Even Go There—
Identifying the Problem

ONE

A Path Beyond Fear

Standing in Stephen Arterburn's office doorway, Maria Taylor looked tense and agitated. The woman walked into his office with a quick, nervous pace, holding her hands in a tight grip. Maria had worked for New Life Ministries for many years and often came by for a quick chat. Stephen smiled and greeted her with a relaxed, "Hi!"

"Sorry to barge in on you like this but I'm obviously upset," Maria began without answering his welcome. She plopped down in the chair in front of the desk. "Nothing's right at our house. I'm afraid Johnny is about to go over the edge and he's got me in total turmoil. I simply don't know what to do."

"Over the edge? I saw him drop you off this morning. He didn't seem to be upset."

"But you didn't talk to him."

"No," Stephen admitted. "I didn't get that close."

"If you had I'm sure you would have noticed how jittery he was. Johnny is that way all the time now. The man has become a walking stick of dynamite."

For a moment Stephen studied Maria's face, trying to decide who was in the worst condition. If Johnny was actually more tense than Maria, he did have a considerable problem. "You seem apprehensive," Stephen observed.

"Apprehensive?" Maria leaned forward in her chair. "Yes, I'm apprehensive, I'm scared to death!"

Obviously, Stephen was dealing with a woman whose fear had swallowed her rationality. Whatever was actually the problem, fright had turned Maria into an emotional wreck. She was clearly in a cold sweat with a case of the shakes. He knew just how she felt. He had been there himself many times. Too many times.

So have most of us. Millions of Americans wake up every morning gripped by the same emotions. Many, many lives would be radically improved if anxious people could find relief from fear, worry, and anxiety. They could see their dreams fulfilled and missions accomplished if they could learn to minimize the paralyzing power of fear. And this is possible!

A week later, Johnny dropped Maria off at work, but this time he came in for his own chat with Stephen. Much to Stephen's surprise, Johnny proved to be even more agitated than Maria had described. As they talked Stephen watched small drops of perspiration form on Johnny's forehead. After ten minutes Stephen noticed Johnny's hand shook slightly. Finally, Johnny blurted out, "I think Maria and I are going to sink financially!"

"Sink?" Stephen drew back. "Johnny, you've retired with a substantial income."

"It won't be enough." Johnny hung his head. "I can see the future clearly now. I think Maria will have to find a better paying job."

"Leave New Life?" Stephen's mouth dropped slightly. He had never had an employee's spouse resign for her.

"Maria can work someplace where our financial needs will be met and we can get by. I don't see any way we can make it through this impending financial crisis."

"Johnny!" Stephen said. "What are you talking about?" He tried to keep his voice under control. He could see why Maria had been so upset.

"We're going to have to put a new roof on the house and it will finish us off. Our financial retirement boat will flip."

Stephen knew Johnny had a handsome retirement check coming every month, and he had several hundred thousand dollars in the bank. The Taylors' home was nearly paid off, and Maria worked because she loved the ministry. Money clearly wasn't the real issue.

Johnny felt as if he was sinking, but the problem was an unidentified, unresolved fear that had become a destructive third member of the Taylor marriage.

In the following weeks, Stephen invited Johnny to come back for some "man-to-man" chats when he brought Maria to work. Stephen explored the source of Johnny's irrational fear and found a troubled childhood. As a result of that uneasy time, Johnny was easily whisked away into a land of terror when the right buttons were punched. Imagination, not fact, had become the monster haunting Johnny Taylor's adult mind. As the men talked, it became apparent that Johnny wasn't much different from countless numbers of people who live daily with the same sense of overwhelming fear haunting their lives, like an outrageous beast ready to pounce mercilessly from a child's dark closet. We all feel it at one time or another.

FEAR IN THE STREETS

On September 11, 2001, America was shaken as terrorist attacks unleashed destruction and death in New York City, in Washington, D.C., and in an open field in Pennsylvania. Millions observed the experiences on television as they actually happened. Hearing the crashing noise of two planes flying directly into the towers of the World Trade Center, seeing balls of fire explode in the air, and watching the walls and floors of the World Trade Center crumble to the ground made Americans violently upset.

As professional counselors across America responded to this avalanche of terror, phone lines at New Life Ministries were jammed, and psychiatrist Paul Meier and Pastor Robert Wise found their own personal counseling schedules filled with clients and parishioners who were struggling to fight back this assault of horror. Throughout the country counselors saw their clients' self-confidence crumble just as the towers had. Many Americans now needed to discover new ways of coping with fear.

The disorder of fear can come in several different packages. Panic has become a highly disabling disorder, leaving millions of Americans emotionally and economically burdened every year. The increase of alcohol and drug abuse in this country bears glaring testimony to the fact that people are looking for exit doors anywhere they can find doorknobs, even if it means an increased dependency on what will prove to be crippling in the long haul.

In addition, phobias plague many people who would never admit to struggling with a disorder. What schizophrenia was in the 1960s, phobias have become in today's society. Victims don't understand how to fight the "what-if" disorder that causes them to become overwhelmed when something triggers the source of their paralyzing fear.

But these may not be the worst problems most of us face!

The Undefined and Unexplained

Many men and women must deal with hazy emotions—the vague yet undefined impression that something is wrong. These victims wake up in the morning with an uneasy sense of dread and go to bed at night with problems still stuck in their minds. Such troubled people wake up in the middle of the night and cannot go back to sleep. The darkest times of evening always hook the darkest side of our personalities and unleash our pent-up emotions. Our dreams rumble and bubble, leaving us trapped by the assaults of our worst terrors. Unable to pinpoint what is happening inside, good people know that "something" bad has its hand on their shoulders.

Decisions are made and cement is poured around life-setting directions without these sufferers facing the fact that their *actions* are actually *a reaction* to unfaced fear. Unless they stand back and rethink what is motivating them, they may spend years racing down the wrong path.

Stephen Arterburn understands well how pervasive this form of mysterious fear can be. He was born with a talent in music, and in his early teenage years, Stephen decided he wanted to be a performer on Broadway. From the age of six he had sung in church, talent shows, local musical productions, and even in a Bob Hope college special. He had studied classical music at Baylor University and received many accolades for his deep baritone voice. He could envision himself standing at the front of a Broadway stage and mesmerizing the audience.

With the sound of imaginary applause ringing in his ears, Stephen set out to get the training and experience that would bring his voice to perfection.

At Baylor he found what he was after—and more. There he received expert instruction, but he also discovered the downside of the entertainment business: the overwhelmingly high failure rate of people who pursued careers in it. He heard endless stories about performers who spent years trying to break through to the bright lights, only to end up with nothing. Such tales slowly eroded Stephen's drive. Without clearly understanding his deepest feelings, Stephen gave up his dreams of Broadway.

Today Stephen clearly understands what shaped his direction in life. He would love to be able to say it was his commitment to God or a desire to serve others, but he admits his whole life was built on a foundation of fear.

Coincidentally, Stephen's radio ministry partner Paul Meier struggled with a similar problem. During his junior-high years, Paul discovered that he too had a good singing voice. His teacher pushed him to sing in the high school choir and finally before the entire student body. As he stood tense but ready to perform before the whole school, Paul opened his mouth and a terrible squeak came out. The student body roared with laughter as Paul desperately wanted to find a drainage ditch to crawl inside and disappear. The experience proved to be devastating.

But Paul fought his fear, and the experience made him determined to sing again. In college, he joined a quartet and received an invitation to sing before a group of a thousand women. Even though eight years had passed, when Paul opened his mouth that night he "squeaked" once more! But with new maturity, he quickly made a joke about the unexpected noise and the women laughed. Paul then confessed, "It's scary to sing in front of so many beautiful women!" They applauded and he relaxed. Fear had turned into forbearance. Today his laughter in the face of difficulty is one of his most enduring characteristics.

Such simple accidents can affect people for a lifetime, leaving them scarred and filled with doubt. This was never our Creator's intention!

GOD'S GIFT: HOPE

At times when a fuzzy feeling of apprehension is sneaking up on us, waiting to explode suddenly like a nuclear bomb killing our dreams, we need to remember what God promised. The Bible is filled with God's pledges of divine intervention, but none is more clear than the apostle Paul's advice to Timothy: "For God did not give us a spirit of timidity, but a spirit of power, of love and of self-discipline" (2 Tim. 1:7 NIV). Christians have the tools to turn back fear!

Rather than using these tools, we often want to live in a world free of fearful situations. When we don't find this, we give up and exist in hopeless desperation. We may even turn away from God because we expected Him to keep us out of harm's way— something God never told us He would do.

Matthew 14 tells a story that clearly illustrates that fearful circumstances may be exactly what God wants for us. The twelve disciples were caught in a dreadful storm and feared for their lives. These same men had walked with Jesus and seen the power of God in action with their own eyes. If there were ever a dozen men who should have been able to face anything with calm and confidence, it was these dozen eggheads who had just that day witnessed God feed five thousand people with a few loaves of bread and several fish. They had watched Jesus feed and heal and teach them the great truths of the universe. Yet, instead of facing their first crisis with courage and godly wisdom, they raised the bar of cowardly behavior to a new level; when Jesus came to help them, they were screaming in terror.

Here is the bottom line of that story. Don't miss it. Even though Jesus knew of the pending storm and the struggle His men would face, *He allowed them* to get into the boat and go out onto that troubled lake.

This amazing story indicates that Jesus may have some lessons to teach us in our difficult times—before He calms the storm and quiets our fears.

If you have given up on God because He did not fulfill your desire to keep you free of all danger and potential disaster, you might want to take a second look at your expectations. God never promised you a trouble-free life. But He does promise to be there with you in the dark times and the stormy seas, to give you hope in spite of fear. This knowledge becomes the foundation for living free of fear's chains.

We have found this to be so in our own lives. Today Stephen Arterburn reaches more people in one day on the New Life radio program than he would have in a lifetime on Broadway. And literally millions of listeners have new hope because they have heeded Paul Meier's advice on this national program. The same hope is available for you.

A ROAD MAP OF WHAT'S AHEAD

In this book we will explore the many forms fear can take. In the first part you'll find help in identifying the problem of fear. We'll take a long look at some of the mysterious noises coming from the dark corners of your own mental attic as well as shine a flashlight on the noises going bump in the night.

In the second section of the book we will focus on discovering answers for the lingering fears that keep haunting us. Phobias, anxiety, insecurities, and panic are only a few of the extreme ways that people find themselves gripped by the cold fingers of fear. You may be surprised that depression can cloak itself as fear. Perhaps, you will discover your fear has worn many disguises, keeping you from the best God planned for your life. You may even be surprised to realize that one source of deep fear—frightening dreams—actually contains good news.

In the final portion of the book, we'll focus on building for the future. We will examine personal and unique areas of apprehension as well as a universal one: the fear of death. We will discuss basic and important ways you can let air out of the fear balloon.

As you read the following chapters, we will take you down a path that can change your responses to the unanticipated experiences happening every day. The new techniques we discuss will provide you with entirely different approaches to transform your haunting problems into new friends. You will find keys to unlock the forbidden doors and open yourself to an entirely changed life of power, love, and self-control. God is waiting to give you the gift of restored hope!

This book is a journey and we are glad you have decided to take it. But since it is a journey, we want to be sure you have the equipment you need: truth as found in the Word of God. Jesus informed and assured us with these words: "Here on earth you will have many trials and sorrows. But take heart, because I have overcome the world" (John 16:33 NLT). We hope you can believe these promises because they are our greatest source of hope. If you can't do so today, we hope you can by the time your journey with this book is over. And we pray it will become the foundation of a life no longer controlled by fear.

TWO

Taking a Peek in
Your Dark Attic

A good portion of Dr. Robert Wise's childhood was spent in the Rocky Mountains. The rippling brook running down Deer Creek Valley and the towering mountains behind the family home fascinated him. He and his sister, Mary, spent the summer months climbing around in the mountains by themselves. Robert particularly loved scampering up the big slopes, finding narrow cracks in gigantic rocks, and edging his way to the top as Mary watched with a terrified stare on her face. The scarier the drop, the better Robert liked it!

Thirty years later Robert sat with a psychologist friend sharing stories over lunch, talking about the crazy things they had done as children. Robert began telling his mountain-climbing stories. After a few moments of thoughtful reflection, his friend asked, "Weren't your parents afraid of the rocks, the heights, the possibility of falling?"

Robert laughed. "They were horrified! I kept them in a nervous twitch every time I started up the mountainside."

"Hmm," the psychologist said. "Is it possible you were actually so reckless because you were trying to deny the reality of their fears? Underneath it all, you were actually afraid?"

The question jolted Robert, leaving him almost speechless. In the middle of a bite from a sandwich, he stopped. Light came flooding in, and he knew the question had hit the bull's-eye. Of course, he had been afraid! More than scaling mountains, he had been trying to climb over his parents' fears.

Our true fears can prove so disconcerting that we deny their existence or find a new label for them. Robert named his fear *recreation;* other people have similar names for their own brands of anxiety. They may live reclusively, assuming this behavior is normal without ever facing the fact that they actually fear someone taking control of their lives. Without any sense of where the attack is coming from, these victims retreat. Robert didn't want to become a victim of what he considered his parents' extreme concern about danger, so he overextended himself, attempting to demonstrate that he wasn't afraid. Robert's daredevil pursuits might have caused him great harm. If he had seen the fear that was really driving him, he would have treated his own safety with more care.

After the terrorist attacks in New York City on September 11, 2001, Dr. Paul Meier started asking his patients about their responses to the destruction. As they talked, he paid close attention to body language. The answers were uniform, expressing fear, grief, outrage, alarm, and many other negative emotions. Many of his patients had flashbacks to other times when they'd felt unexpectedly terrified.

Paul's patients' pain, combined with his own pain, took its toll on him. He talked about his dismay and doubts with his wife, his children, and his colleagues. For years he had handled each day with objective compassion. September 11 erased that objectivity, and Paul now associated too deeply with his patients' fears. As he realized this, Paul found his tenseness gradually dissipating.

It's important for us to be able to know when fear has captured us, so we can act appropriately when we feel the prison doors of fear clanging shut. God's design is apparent in the Scripture we mentioned in chapter 1. He didn't create a spirit of fear in us, but one of power, love, and self-control (2 Tim. 1:7).

Often the word *fear* is translated "timidity." Interestingly enough, timid people may not think of themselves as being afraid, but they are actually quiet because they're apprehensive about how other people will receive them. God didn't plan for us to live under the cloud of such qualms. His intention was that we live happy, connected lives, free from intimidation. No matter what our source of fear, God wants us to learn how to minimize its power over us.

THE DIFFERENT FACES OF FEAR

As we've seen, fear can disguise itself behind many masks. Often the person who is controlled by fear is unaware of how fear is manifested in daily living. The following nine statements symbolize a fear-controlled life. As you ponder these possibilities, place a check mark beside the statements that sound like you.

_____ *"I have a fear of losing control."*

Dysfunctional families often produce adults who feel that life is constantly spinning out of control. As a consequence, these people develop perfectionistic behavior to help them compensate for the chaos. They try to control every detail of life to quiet the sense of impending disaster that they grew up with. While they may be nice, accommodating people when others are in difficulty, these troubled folks will have difficulty admitting their own struggles and avoid asking for help.

Perfectionists are people who take longer to order in restaurants for fear of making mistakes. They may sit with their backs to the wall so they can feel more in control of the room. In church or at the movies, they like to sit on the aisle so they won't feel trapped. Rejection of people is easy because so many just don't measure up.

A tough childhood isn't the only source of this tendency. Sometimes a small fear spins into a bigger one, and for many reasons people can't stop the escalation. Without reflecting on their problem, they turn into "control freaks."

_____ *"I feel I live in a different world from everyone else."*

Ever feel unreal, numb, or think you are losing your mind? During a panic attack people may feel they are outside of their bodies, looking in on what is happening around them. Those feelings are aspects of depersonalization.

This condition follows when one's sense of identity is displaced. Robert Wise was adopted as a child, and because he did not identify with the family he was placed with, he still struggles with who he is. Sufferers no longer relate to family members or colleagues as if they are part of the same human race. They may feel as if they are going through an identity crisis.

Pressures can push us out of our comfort zone and we lose our grasp on what is real. We overreact to such an extent we lose our emotional sense of having any grip on the situation at hand. Fear takes over and we withdraw.

_____ *"I feel that death may be imminent."*

No normal person wants to die! Fear is an inherent and natural concern for physical well-being. However, normal apprehension can turn into our enemy. Pushed far enough, anxiety can become a dread that life is slipping away. Extreme fear can even become the conviction that death is imminent.

We may find ourselves thinking about death too often. Possibly our behavior has become so defensive it inhibits our normal performance. Illness becomes larger than life. As victims of fear, we begin to suspect that awful diseases like cancer are already attacking us and our death is just ahead. Dying becomes a constant and haunting terror, popping up in our thinking all the time.

_____ *"I often feel as if I may never be able to catch my breath."*

Fear doesn't stay in our heads but runs through our bodies much like our bloodstream. The irrational and uncontrollable spread of apprehension reaches inside our nervous system and throws control switches by its own power. Fright makes our hearts beat faster and we need more oxygen. Breathing naturally increases. A sudden frightening experience can make our chest muscles tighten and our throat constrict. These normal muscular sensations add to the impact of fear and matters quickly get worse.

Shortness of breath won't kill anybody but we can feel like it's a genuine possibility. As fear progresses, we often feel unsteady and faint, and we have to sit down so we won't fall down. Our heart pounds furiously, and we may become certain we will die!

These symptoms are caused by the powerful vagus nerve, which begins in the brain, runs down the spinal cord, and extends throughout the body. It has branches running to the heart, the visceral region, and up to blood vessels as well as the skin. This nerve transmits the effects of anxiety and can cause a knee-jerk reaction throughout the body. Once the nervous system goes into overload, our bodies have a natural physiology we can't control rationally. Dizziness develops when our internal system is telling us we have pushed ourselves beyond our limits.

_____"*I feel pain around my heart or that it is beating out of control.*"

When your heart beats harder, you are struggling with palpitations; when it beats faster, you are experiencing tachycardia. While either symptom is a problem, neither is an immediate cause for extreme concern. However, people experiencing these symptoms because of anxiety frequently fly into an emergency room, certain they are having a heart attack. Even when they find out otherwise, the experience confirms their fear that life may be spinning out of control.

_____"*I am self-conscious about my trembling hands, sweaty palms, and chills.*"

In addition to perspiration, frightened people may experience sudden hot flashes arising from the overload created by fear. The throat may tighten. A fit of choking follows, but the source of the problem is still the overstimulated vagus nerve.

Red blotches may appear on the face or the neck where anxiety has caused a release of histamine into our system. Or chills make us feel like someone has dropped us into a refrigerator, but the source of the sensation is emotion.

_____"*I feel inexplicably nauseous.*"

A shock can cause frightened persons to develop nausea. Fear can stimulate our gastric system to such an extent that subtle flip-flops turn into significant problems. Cramps, ulcers, and even ulcerative colitis can result.

You may feel like suddenly running to the nearest bathroom. Or you may just feel a rumbling in your stomach or become slightly queasy when gripped by fear. The problem isn't what you ate—it's what's eating you.

_____*"I feel my hands or feet going numb or feel a tingling sensation."*
Any part of the body can become numb or develop a tingling sensation after an emotional shock. Anxiety can affect all the nerves in the body and play tremendous tricks on people. Sufferers can become paralyzed, mute, or blind from nothing more than fear.

_____*"I feel like my chest is thick, heavy, and painful."*
Doctors know there is a significant difference between a genuine heart attack and chest pain. If we feel as if someone has placed a rock on our chest and the pain starts radiating toward our left arm, the chances are good that we are experiencing the real thing! Panic produces a different sensation. A sudden sharp pain in the chest is caused when the muscles between our ribs contract in a "charley horse" reaction. The pain doesn't radiate but gets worse when we take a deep breath. While the difference is significant, it is still worthwhile to check out the problem medically.

A word of warning! Don't be alarmed if you discover some of these symptoms floating around in your world. Everyone has a few of these aspects of fear in their lives. It's normal. However, having a majority or all of these factors might indicate that you could be a victim of your fears and could benefit from the liberating truth of God's Word.

In fact, some who struggle with fear don't experience any of these symptoms. Instead they may feel a simple discomfort or unease in any situation. That constant feeling of uncertainty is described in James 1:6: "unsettled as a wave of the sea that is driven and tossed by the wind" (NLT). Every day is this person's own constant storm. If any of this describes you, there is hope.

FIVE POSSIBILITIES FOR THE FEARFUL

We don't want to wait until the end of the book to help you resolve your fears. So here are some possibilities that can help you settle down, relax, and finish the book.

Knowing the symptoms and some of the body's reactions will help you become more realistic about your fears. In addition, you may need to take some important, specific steps to subdue any fears of being out of control. When you recognize the icy fingers of fear digging into your shoulder, try these five practical strategies.

1. Face Your Fear

You need to open your locked closet and let the sunlight in. You can't get well unless you confront the facts. The *fear of your fear* can sometimes be the biggest problem you face. As you read the following chapters, you will find many different approaches to getting honest with yourself about your feelings. Taking a peek into your dark attic can be one of your most important steps toward sound mental health.

2. Set Boundaries

Learn to say no! Drs. John Townsend and Henry Cloud wrote a book, *Boundaries*, that revolutionized practical Christianity. Their Boundaries series (*Boundaries with Kids, Boundaries in Marriage*) has helped millions of people both directly and indirectly. In the books the doctors make the point that everyone needs to set parameters. Creating limits keeps us out of the places where destructiveness happens. Learning to say no is one of the most important boundaries that will keep us out of harm's way.

Many people find this change to be a particularly difficult step because they have become conditioned to saying yes to every request and they are afraid to say no. Refusing feels inconsiderate or impertinent. Consequently, these victims go from problem to problem without realizing that they keep opening the door to their own difficulties. And the fear of disappointing someone controls them.

3. Consider Insight-Oriented Therapy

We must learn to face and resolve old losses and stresses. Often we need help in working through these unresolved issues. Don't feel weak for needing help. Feel strong for asking for it. Scripture reminds us: "Plans fail for lack of counsel,/ but with many advisers they succeed" (Prov. 15:22 NIV). Professional help can make all the difference in getting to the bottom of our fears.

4. Consider Medication

In the right combinations, medications work nearly 100 percent of the time. While most of the people who seek professional help are able to overcome their fears through counseling alone, many times panic-stricken patients need a physiological, chemical change that will enable them to resolve their fear-related issues. Dr. Meier recognizes that spiritual issues often lie behind the cause of apprehension, and patients must deal with these in conjunction with medication if they are going to become totally whole. He insists that people see a good Christian counselor and not just expect a quick fix from taking a pill.

People give many reasons for not considering medication. One of the central objections is that "I should be able to handle and resolve problems on my own." Many fear-struck strugglers have gone to an early grave with that naive belief, when in reality God had a gift available for them. They only needed to humble themselves enough to take it.

5. Connect

We need to be connected to God and His people. Spending time with loving, grace-filled servants of God can soothe anyone's fear. Unconditional love is healing and will help us maintain perspective. New hope and direction can come from establishing positive relationships with people to whom we can confess our fears.

Sometimes we have missed the reasons why we feel so disconnected and alienated. Exploring the strained relationships of the past can cut these unhealthy ties. You may need to spend time looking at what destroyed your past relationships.

Most important of all is to come into a new, intimate relationship with our heavenly Father. He's the One who has the capacity and potential to restore our lives and is waiting to do so. A revived relationship with Jesus Christ can add the power and opportunity needed to reconnect with people and God—and to face fear.

Remember that God's gifts are power, love, and self-control. But you won't experience them unless you work through all the reasons you have become disconnected from the Father. He is the ultimate, healing connection.

THREE

Things That Go Bump in the Night

Karen Richards's troubled childhood started with her mother's difficult marriage. The resulting divorce pushed the family into financial hardship and forced seventeen-year-old Karen to take a job, working as a chore woman in a local motel. The attractive young girl cleaned, straightened, and made beds. She didn't mind the work, but she soon learned to be leery of the guests. Men often tried to corner her, and despite her precautions, Karen faced the degrading and humiliating experiences of sexual abuse. Afraid she had done something to bring on the attacks, Karen kept her molestation a secret. After two years Karen finally left the motel job, feeling alone, guilty, and afraid.

Carrying an unbearable load of guilt she couldn't express to anyone, Karen turned to a local church where a kind fellow struggler befriended her and led her to a personal relationship with Christ. Although she had not done anything wrong, she felt the same shame so many victims feel. She knew the promise of forgiveness applied to her, but she couldn't seem to let it penetrate the hidden realm of her memories.

Years passed, and Karen met a man she deeply loved and a good marriage followed. She attended college and studied to become a teacher. Her adventures in teaching and marriage seemed to have forever blotted out the old experiences back in the motel.

One afternoon Karen had to stay for a conversation with the school principal to talk about the business of the classroom. The man got up and walked across the office, shutting the front door. Karen heard the lock click and felt a cold sense of dread. She kept talking but knew the principal was walking up behind her. Suddenly he grabbed her just as the men in the motel had done in the past. Karen struggled to avoid his grip but couldn't fight him off.

Suddenly the locked door of Karen's memory was ripped off the hinges. What had been buried erupted with terrifying fury. Even though she had broken free from the cruel man, her anxiety ate into her mind, leaving her trapped in haunting depression.

Each day slowly dragged by, but Karen didn't improve. The blackness of fear covered her like a shroud, immobilizing her ability to make sound decisions. At night she found it difficult to sleep and she often awoke feeling worn out. Her appetite fell off and she began to withdraw. An awful sense of gnawing depression infected everything Karen tried to do. Finally, one night she couldn't stand the pain any longer.

Staggering out to her car, Karen started down the road, driving faster and faster. A single idea gripped her mind. She wanted to die. An old bridge with a big metal abutment stood not far from town. Karen reckoned she could hit the steel structure head-on at a high rate of speed and end her life.

Karen no longer felt any power was left inside. She flew down the highway ready to end her life. Dying definitely seemed preferable to living. She held the steering wheel carefully and aimed the car at the bridge.

At that moment something strange happened. As Karen tried to adjust the steering wheel, nothing moved. The car had always been kept in good maintenance but for some unexplainable reason the wheel locked. Karen tried to wrench it free but she couldn't budge the direction of the car. No matter what she tried, the car wasn't going to hit the bridge!

Instead of striking the abutment, Karen's car careened into the ditch and flipped over. The terrible roar of the engine echoed in her ears as her head pounded against the glass window and into the steering wheel. With a terrible crashing sound, the car came to rest against the side of the ditch. Karen was only semiconscious and could hear little except the sound of glass falling out of the shattered windows. Without Karen's touching anything, the car radio abruptly came on. She blinked several times, trying to focus on the sounds arising from the speaker. Slowly Karen began to realize the radio was tuned to a Christian station. After a few moments, she recognized the song as an old familiar church hymn promising God's help "up from the ashes." The words offered Karen hope that out of the burnt places of her pain and abuse, God wanted to reshape and remold her life.

Karen couldn't believe what she was hearing. She hadn't touched the radio knobs, yet out of the thin air a Christian station offered a voice from heaven. She couldn't avoid facing the fact that God's love, forgiveness, and grace had saved her life!

LEARNING HOW TO USE FEAR

Karen Richards's struggle developed from an inability to place painful events in their right place and not allow attackers to gain control over her life.

As we've seen in Karen's story, unresolved fear doesn't disappear with time. Christian counselors know the impact of allowing anxiety to hide in the crevices of one's mind: fear actually expands and grows in the darkness, exploding later with life-shattering force. The ministry of counselors like Arterburn, Meier, and Wise helps troubled persons get in touch with their old, hidden fears so that the pieces can be pulled to the surface and exposed to the light of day. Only then can the fullness of the promises of Jesus Christ be released to heal the past.

There's a lesson here that Karen hadn't learned. The men in the motel treated her like an animal, instilling fear in her soul. Karen wasn't able to grasp that many of the men were motivated far more by a need to be in control than to have a sexual conquest. The basic issue was power! Often in our civilized world, people use verbal, physical, and even sexual abuse as a way to terrorize others. Such behavior often makes the perpetrator feel powerful while defeating his victim.

Despite such realities, the Bible makes it clear that we are to fear God, not other human beings. Jesus said, "Do not be afraid of those who kill the body but cannot kill the soul" (Matt. 10:28 NIV). We need to develop an ability to keep people in the right perspective. Genesis 14 tells the story of Abraham's anger when he discovered that a fearful Lot and his family had been taken prisoners by the Elamite army. In contrast, Abraham fearlessly gathered his forces and chased the entire Elamite army until he obtained the release of his relatives. He was bold because God had revealed to Abraham through a vision that he was not to be afraid of other people; instead he should rely on the divine protection extended to him. Christians can live with the same confidence. God intends that we be equipped with an awareness of His care, liberating us from apprehensions about other people.

All of us have a basic need to identify what we are afraid of and learn to respond in a creative, not negative, manner. Often people are actually afraid of good things, such as giving love or being loved. Fear should teach us where we should make detours; it shouldn't keep us from living at all.

TURNING FEAR INTO GOOD FORTUNE

God wanted to do more for Karen than only heal yesterday's pain. He wanted to start her on a whole new life.

Karen Richards returned home from the hospital in a battered and frightened condition. Fortunately, she had not broken any bones and had only been cut around her face and arms. The only lingering signs of the wreck were the bandages and bruises. She knew something awesome had occurred to keep her car wreck from being fatal, but couldn't put the pieces of the scattered puzzle together. Then her telephone rang.

"This is Dr. Harris," the family's physician said. "I'm very concerned about you, Karen. Since I saw you at the hospital I've been thinking about this smashup. The wreck could have taken your life."

"Yes," Karen said weakly.

"I want you to see a friend of mine . . . a psychiatrist in Dallas, Texas."

"But—" Karen started to object.

The physician cut her off. "Yes, I know finances are always tight after a wreck. So, I'm paying all the costs and expenses. You will be in the clinic for several weeks as Dr. Meier helps you work your way through the things that are troubling you. I want you to leave tomorrow morning."

Karen hung up in a daze. She felt she had no choice but to

accept what the doctor had offered. She started packing for her long trip to Texas. Her husband felt this trip was the right decision and encouraged Karen to go. The next day he drove her to the airport.

—✦—

During the next four weeks, Dr. Meier worked with Karen on a daily basis, helping her to face the truth and release the pain and hostility that held her captive. After a few sessions Karen's basic fear emerged. Since her childhood, she had always been afraid of her own rage and of losing control of her emotions. Anger and hostility might overpower her and make her crazy, she thought. This fear, along with her dread of people who might hurt her, had created the penal system that had locked Karen in an emotional dungeon and set up her breakdown. Through counseling, group therapy, insight-oriented therapy, and deep loving care, Dr. Meier helped Karen get in touch with her emotions, grieve, put those apprehensions behind her, and discover a new way to live. Dr. Meier has found that four simple decisions have helped multitudes of patients. He often leads his patients in this basic life commitment and offered the following pledge to Karen:

1. Decide to Become Like Christ

Commit yourself to the dynamic, loving qualities you find in Jesus Christ and make a decision to become like Him.

2. Serve Christ

Make your highest objective to serve Jesus Christ in all of your relationships and circumstances. Replace fear with a commitment to care.

3. Stay Out of Trouble

Many people don't stop and reflect before they make important decisions. Simply avoiding pitfalls can do wonders to end the negative work of fear in our lives.

4. Learn and Grow from Whatever Goes Wrong Each Day

Pay attention to where you stumbled and don't do it again. When unexpected troubles hit, learn and grow from these disappointments, becoming a better and more mature human being.

Like many patients before her, Karen found another life was possible. With fresh determination she decided to walk down this new path.

A few weeks later, Paul watched Karen walk out of the clinic. She had come in looking like a beaten animal, but Karen left with her face set against the wind. She eventually returned to the university and obtained her master's degree in counseling. With her increased skills in personal dynamics and group work, Karen drew the attention of an international missions and ministry organization. The organization hired her, and in short time, Karen Richards became the director of this worldwide endeavor. Karen had learned to understand and use fear constructively.

You might read a story like Karen's and think that God is at work in everyone's life but yours. Or you may think that once you "get fixed" God will use you as He is using Karen. But we want you to know that God is at work in your life right now as you read this. And He wants you to work with Him now, even as you begin to deal with your fears.

What is most reassuring to all of us who struggle is the fact that the apostle Paul had a huge, unresolved problem. That problem was so severe that Paul called it "a messenger from Satan." (Ever feel like your fears were directly from Satan?) And Paul's problem was so bad, he used the word *torment* to describe its effect on him. Paul begged God to take this problem away, yet God did not. Instead God told Paul, "My gracious favor is all you need. My power works best in your weakness" (2 Cor. 12:7, 9 NLT).

If Paul had waited for God to remove his horrible problem before he journeyed throughout the Mediterranean to tell others about Christ, this world might have been very different.

From his experience we can draw some very important conclusions. First, even people God uses are not trouble-free. They struggle as all of us do. Second, God wants to use us as we are. Finally, the weaker we are, the stronger God's power can be in our lives.

We close this chapter with God's words of encouragement for you. Isaiah 40:28–31 says,

> Do you not know? Have you not heard?
> The Everlasting God, the LORD, the Creator
>   of the ends of the earth
> Does not become weary or tired.
> His understanding is inscrutable.
> He gives strength to the weary,
> And to him who lacks might He increases power.
> Though youths grow weary and tired,
> And vigorous young men stumble badly,
> Yet those who wait for the LORD
> Will gain new strength;
> They will mount up with wings like eagles,
> They will run and not get tired,
> They will walk and not become weary.

Could it be time for you to fly?

FOUR

Stumbling Block
or Stepping-Stone?

You can live beyond your fear!

Sure, it's easy to make fear sound like our enemy, but the feeling did begin as a gift from God. Failure to appreciate the possibilities of fear is part of what positions us for trouble. We make an enemy out of what should be our friend. While misapplied fear can wreck us, *fear is actually power!*

The Bible tells us that the fear of God is the beginning of wisdom (Prov. 1:7). Reverent awareness of who God is, His power, and His plans for the world is the beginning of intelligence. We are able to recognize the proper relationship between humans and animals, between humans and other humans, and between us and our Creator.

In the story of Noah and his family, the book of Genesis relates that after the great Flood God placed a fear of humans in all animals, birds, and fish (Gen. 9:2). The result? People could live beyond their fear of great beasts and thereby gained power over creation; we automatically had more control than our strength would normally have afforded us because of the animals' apprehension.

Our need is to learn how to release the power latent in our fears.

Ships' logs written by captains sailing in Polynesian waters in the seventeenth century reveal how powerful irrational fear can be. During those years, many captains recorded how their meager crews, starving, weak, and without water, could sail up to an island occupied by thousands of strong natives and within minutes take control of tribes that normally killed every intruder. The sailors could do this because the natives had never seen white skin, and they were afraid of these white men.

Like the natives, you may be afraid of what you don't understand.

Once the natives realized that the color of skin did not make these sailors gods, the natives killed them. And once you finally understand your fears, there is a good possibility you will destroy them.

BLIND TO THE PROMISE

Dr. Meier watched the orderly lead Sharon Anderson into his hospital office. Sharon took each step with a careful, hesitating gait. She constantly reached in front of herself, groping to make sure she hit nothing. This bright college student, who made good grades at Harvard and had always been a highly capable person, was now inexplicably blind.

Paul glanced at Sharon's medical chart. The best doctors and neurologists on the Harvard Medical School staff had examined her, and not one had been able to identify any medical reason for her blindness. Overnight she simply lost her sight and was eventually referred to Dr. Meier for psychiatric care.

Paul watched the orderly help Sharon sit down. Each fearful movement typified patients with recent loss of vision.

After the first hour's examination, Dr. Meier realized Sharon had no insight into her blindness or her personal problems. She was as mystified about her lack of vision as the neurologist had been. Paul immediately saw the need for a radical change in Sharon's environment. He suggested the staff do nothing to support her blindness. No rewards for the problem! If Sharon tripped and fell, no one could pick her up or assist her in any way.

On the other hand, Sharon received instant affirmation when she openly shared her problems and thoughts during the counseling process. She admitted that even though she grew up in a family that looked good on the outside, serious problems existed at the core. Early in her childhood, Sharon discovered that her mother, Joyce, had been running around on her father. Joyce's unfaithful behavior split her daughter's emotions. On one side, she loved her mother and only wanted the best for her; but on the other Sharon hated what her mother had done. Like an ax cutting firewood, ambivalence split Sharon's soul; she was both drawn to her mother and repelled by her.

During counseling sessions Paul learned that something highly significant had occurred just before the onset of Sharon's blindness. Her mother had called her at Harvard and told her that the family doctor had just discovered she had incurable cancer, with only six months to live. She needed Sharon to come home and take care of her as death approached.

Dr. Meier instantly recognized what Sharon had carefully avoided. She had never faced the ambivalence she felt toward her mother. She wanted to help her mother, even though dropping out of college for six months obviously pained her. Yet part of her did not want to see Joyce at all. Even though she wouldn't have called it fear, Sharon was afraid to face her apprehensions in a straightforward way. Her mind had created the blindness so she wouldn't have to face the love/hate relationship she had with her mother.

Several weeks passed as Dr. Meier worked with Sharon on these issues. Paul sensed that she had started looking more candidly at her apprehensions and was beginning to understand how her life was inwardly divided against itself. He also believed Sharon might be coming to the place where her unconscious mind was ready to give up blindness as a defense against facing the war going on inside her. Paul decided to try an unusual approach: the power of suggestion.

"Sharon," Dr. Meier began, "I believe you are coming to a turning point. Is that possible?"

Sharon nodded her head. "Yes," she said thoughtfully, "I believe I've learned a great deal in the last several weeks."

"I think you're ready to release your blindness. I want you to lie down and take a nap. When you wake up, your sight will have returned. Okay? Your eyes will see."

"I'm willing to try. Let's see what happens."

Paul stood up. "I'm going home now. Stretch out and make yourself comfortable." He started walking toward the door. "See you later."

While Paul wasn't certain, he felt the power of suggestion would be significant enough to break the emotional chains keeping Sharon's eyes shut. He drove home in a hopeful mood. An hour and a half later the telephone rang.

"Dr. Meier!" the nurse shouted. "We've had a miracle!"

"What?"

"Sharon! Sharon Anderson's sight returned. She's just walked down the hall with her vision fully restored. It's a miracle!"

"No." Paul laughed. "No, this one isn't a divine intervention but a patient getting honest about her emotions. She's finally understood what was driving her blindness."

All of us can make the same decision to understand our fears.

Sharon had every right to be angry about her mother's adultery. Not only was the behavior immoral, but it hurt everyone in the family. However, she wouldn't admit her feelings about her mother so she could deal with them directly. Once she understood that fear was driving her blindness, she was able to overcome this irrational response.

Sharon's fear was irrational, but some fears are quite rational.

A TIME TO BE AFRAID!

Many times every day, we need to be alert to avoid disasters; there are times when we should be afraid. The Bible tells us to avoid dangerous pitfalls. In fact, the fourth chapter of the book of Judges tells a story about the importance of maintaining a cautious perspective.

The entire period of the judges proved to be one of Israel's most difficult historical episodes. Moral confusion abounded and "every man did what was right in his own eyes" (Judg. 17:6). During one of the times of moral confusion, the forces of Sisera bore down on the nation of Israel, threatening to annihilate the Israelites on Mount Tabor. Judge Deborah urged the Jewish leader Barak not to be afraid because God had given them the victory. The people of Israel had repented of their sin, sought the face of God, and the Almighty would answer. The soldiers of Sisera soon fell to the sword, and Sisera ran for his life.

As Sisera fled, he sought a place of shelter. Ignoring the fact that he should be afraid of entering the tent of a civilian Israelite, Sisera went in for a nap. While he was sleeping, Jael grabbed a stake and drove it through his temple, killing the Canaanite general. Fear would have been *very* constructive!

NEW BUILDING UNDER WAY

At this moment, there's a good possibility you are struggling with some fears in your own life. You may be highly aware of them or, like Sharon Anderson, you may not, but as you read the next few paragraphs please keep thinking about your personal fears. Ask yourself how these problems could become stepping-stones for the future.

As you probe your fears, you will probably wonder what you can do to correct the problems. Where could you find help to make a significant difference? Here are three steps you can take to help you build an emotionally sound life.

1. Face the Fear

We naturally avoid the pain associated with our apprehensions. That's understandable—but not constructive!

Make a resolution to start facing the cause of your shivers. Once you consciously make the decision, new gears start moving in your unconscious mind. Wheels turn and doors open. Light breaks into the darkness and insight follows. The depth of your own ability to understand yourself may surprise you.

What fears are you facing right now? Write those fears in the space below:

2. Look for an Alternative

Fear represents healthy concern. Your job is to let fear do its best work, which keeps you out of trouble. However, your apprehension can take you in the wrong direction. Substituting a new road map for the old one you've been using can take you to the place of peace you need to find. What's the alternative to what you're worrying about *right now*? Think about it.

For example, if you're afraid of heights and must walk across a stairway bridge three stories off the ground to reach your office at work every day, you've got a problem. You need to find an alternative to your fear of heights. Will you find an elevator? Close your eyes and have a friend lead you across? Start facing your emotional response in a different way? Your answers form possible alternative responses.

What are some new possibilities for using your fears in a different manner? Find a more constructive way to go and write it in the space below. (For example, if you have a legitimate fear of someone attacking you when you are walking through a dark parking garage, get a purse-sized container of mace and carry the weapon with you. The idea is to find a new way to make your fear work for you.)

Reflect on what you've written. How does it look? Do you feel good about the possibilities? Think them over several times and then ask God to help you get beyond your fear.

3. Pray About New Direction

Fear often isolates us. Without reflection, we may feel we're all we've got left! Emptiness is frightening. Loneliness multiplies the impact of fear and we no longer see or believe that any hope remains. Boom! We're lost. When we are sure no one is walking with us, a difficult route feels impossible to navigate.

Prayer puts us back in touch with the fact we are never alone. God always stands in the shadows, available to help us walk across the empty valley. His strong arm lifts what we thought we couldn't carry and gives us extraordinary capacity. Abruptly, we're on our way to a new day! No matter what alternatives you are considering, make them a matter of intercession.

A Final Thought

Keep in mind the fact that *fear is power!* Our apprehensions always carry a latent capacity for us to take control of situations that would otherwise cause us to retreat. The need is to release the capacities that God has given us in this awesome force. Remember: you *can* move beyond your fears. And you can make them stepping-stones rather than stumbling blocks.

PART 2

Turning Crisis into Confidence – Discovering Answers

FIVE

The Launching Pad

How can you change the impact of fear on your life? Having taken a brief look at the problem of fear, we need to consider the origin of our troublesome behaviors and how we can find relief from their intrusion in our lives.

Dr. Paul Meier discovered he had a fear of failure as well as a fear of *not* failing! Sound dichotomous? It is! Remember Paul's problem with his voice squeaking when he tried to sing? Another strange and unexpected form of the problem appeared immediately after the Moody Broadcasting Network invited Drs. Paul Meier and Frank Minirth to start their own live talk show to a nationwide audience of at least a million listeners. The first show started with a listener calling in.

"Please, Dr. Meier," the anonymous caller began, "how can I face my fear of closed spaces?"

"Well, ma'am," Paul answered, "there are three things you can do with that problem. First, you need to look at where the fear began." Suddenly, Paul's mind went blank. Whatever he had intended to suggest was gone. He stared helplessly at Frank Minirth. At that moment Paul realized he couldn't even recall the woman's question. Paul's memories of his squeaky singing probably triggered a mental response, and he abruptly went blank.

"Let me add a thought." Dr. Minirth immediately picked up the conversation and kept talking until Paul recovered. Slumped back in his chair, Paul stared at the microphone. Panic had erased every thought in his head!

Where in the world did those squeaks, squawks, and blanks come from?

Looking Backward

Paul started searching to find the source of what had thrown the wrench in his mental machinery. He knew it was necessary to look at the past. This exploration produced the strange paradox of his both wanting and not wanting to fail.

Paul's earliest memory proved to be a fear of losing either his father's or mother's approval. Growing up in a family in which he was the middle child, Paul faced the normal peer pressures his older siblings did, but he responded to this pressure by doing everything humanly possible to please his parents, to the point of becoming compliant with their every expectation. By the time he went to grade school, Paul was already set to do precisely what they desired.

Soon he was knocking down As and rare Bs and doing exceptionally well—except at home. Alexander Meier, Paul's father, would examine his report card carefully, noting the occasional Bs.

"Why didn't you get an A?" his father asked, pointing at the B+ on the report.

"I—I—guess I didn't try hard enough," Paul stammered. "I'll do better next time."

"Good!" Alexander answered dogmatically. "I expect the best

from my son. I know you can get all As. Go back in there and try harder."

While intending to encourage his son, Alexander Meier was actually reinforcing Paul's fear of failure. Good grades appeared to be at the top of Alexander's list. Perfect papers were the only acceptable order of the day.

At school Paul discovered the other side of the coin. Being smart was not "cool." When he was the first to turn in his test or raise his hand to answer the teacher's question, Paul faced being ostracized by other students. He might be the winner of the day at home but his peers considered him to be the loser of the week. Paul had to adjust his behavior and quickly found new ways to create an accepting atmosphere in the classroom. He made sure at least two other students had already turned in their test answers before dropping his paper on the teacher's desk. Paul learned to get laughs by acting stupid when actually he was one of the most intelligent kids in the class. He needed to fail to gain the approval of his peers.

But the need went deeper.

Paul secretly wanted to punish his father for expecting too much from him. He needed to fail to settle the score with Dad!

And this is what Satan wanted Paul to do. This goes directly against a principle found in Hebrews 13: "We confidently say, 'The Lord is my helper, I will not be afraid. What shall man do to me?'" (v. 6). We realize that this is easier said than done, but when we focus on God being for us, we eliminate the power any man has against us. If Paul could have replaced his father's disapproval with God's love for him, he would have found no need to even the score.

In your own life, there is no need to even the score. Allow God to take care of the score while you simply play the game by His rules. His rules are never mean, cruel, or legalistic.

Legalism Disguised as Piety

Many times well-meaning Christians grow up with a strict form of the Christian faith that automatically sets them up for problems. Teachers and parents communicate, *"If you break the rules, God will get you!"*

The Meiers' home was a legalistic setting where rule keeping was all-important. No use of scissors on Sunday, lest Paul break the Sabbath. Using "real" cards was evil! (Rook cards were different, you understand.) Square dancing in elementary school had to be wrong because any form of dancing was sinful, and Paul couldn't attend those Disney movies about Bambi and Mickey Mouse because theaters were "the devil's workshop." Using any form of alcohol was wrong; his parents explained that Jesus' first miracle of turning water into wine actually resulted in nonalcoholic grape juice, not wine. All this talk about keeping rigid rules added to Paul's fear of failure.

Later, after Paul graduated from medical school and finished his psychiatry residency, he taught and counseled students at Dallas Theological Seminary. There he noticed an interesting spin-off of the same problem. Paul noted that hundreds of students scored above average on psychological tests that measured their desires to be conscientious and moral. At the same time, they scored equally higher than normal on their need to rebel, fail, and be morally deviant. The contradiction reflected their internal struggle in dealing with failure.

Paul had learned from his psychiatry professors at Duke University that one out of every four ministers in the United States has an affair with a church member. At the same time, only one out of twenty (usually nonreligious) practicing psychiatrists fail in a moral relationship with patients. Obviously, many well-motivated believers have not understood that rigid attention to following rules is part of an unexamined fear of failure and can still lead to failure.

Stephen Arterburn grew up in a similar environment but it produced a different type of fear. In Stephen's family, abstaining from alcohol was also a premier value. Stephen asked his father, "Why would Jesus make turning water into wine His first miracle if it was so bad?" His father replied, "Well, if He had known how many problems alcohol would cause, He never would have done that." We don't think Steve's father had fully thought that answer through, but it was just one instance of making the world fit around a set of do's and don'ts—mostly don'ts.

As Stephen grew up, the only Christians he knew were weird rule keepers. At the time Christian television looked more like a freak show than a reflection of healthy spirituality. Stephen's personal fear was looking like a weirdo. He did whatever he could so he would not be pigeonholed into a caricature of Christ. Amazingly, that fear led to New Life Ministries being a place where people could be real as well as a place where fake Christians are not honored.

Have you spent time looking at the weird things and people in your past? Might these be the source of your obsessive fears?

FIGURING OUT THE PROBLEM

Many times we get stuck trying to unravel how we developed compulsive behaviors. What's lurking at the bottom of the problem looks like a dark gas bubble popping in a tar pit. Nothing is clear.

Whether our voices have or have not squeaked, we need to

discover how to get to the base level of our fear problem, just as Dr. Meier did. Let's look at a method Steve Arterburn often uses in his seminars and institutes. It is important to look at this in light of Galatians 5:22–24. In this passage the apostle Paul directed us to crucify our passions and desires so that the Holy Spirit—not our compulsions and fears—will control our lives.

In order to understand the murkiness, take a piece of paper or use the area below to note a behavior that's been bothering you. Across the top of the paper, write out these three headings. The page should look like this:

RESULTING COMPULSION	UNDERLYING OBSESSION	UNRESOLVED FEAR
1.		
2.		
3.		

For a few moments, look at the first column. Can you identify any actions in your life that might be compulsive behaviors? Eating? Working? Saving money? Trying to please? Lay the book down for a few minutes and give careful thought to how you consistently perform every day of the week. Do you see repetitious patterns? A few more areas to consider are shopping, shoplifting, lying, drinking, exercising, engaging in pre- or extramarital sex, and masturbation. Write down each compulsive behavior you identify.

Digging Deeper

In order to get a handle on how fear may be twisting your life into unpleasant configurations, you must start with your current behavior and work backward to the source of the problem. Here are some examples to get you started.

RESULTING COMPULSION	UNDERLYING OBSESSION	UNRESOLVED FEAR
1. "Looking for love in all the wrong places" or compulsive sexual acts	love	
2. Being constantly ill or worrying about eliminating germs from your life	health, health foods	
3. Domineering, controlling, perfectionistic behavior	maintaining order	

These three compulsions are quite common in today's world. Everyone knows friends who inevitably end up in relationships that break their hearts. Look at the second group, those who are constantly ill. They go from symptom to symptom and from doctor to doctor. There's a different type of problem in the third category—controlling persons attempt to dominate everyone around them. These people send us running, unless we want to be controlled!

In each of these incidences of compulsive behavior, we have identified an obsession. For example, unwise lovers are so possessed with their need for love that they misunderstand the urgency of their own compulsion. They are hardly out of one relationship before they are jumping into the next. Moving so quickly that reflection isn't possible, these needy persons leap disastrously from person to person. They have moved from a healthy desire to have their needs met to an unhealthy neediness.

Similarly, hypochondriacs bounce from ulcers to sinus problems and then on to arthritis—whatever's trendy. Often they are experts in the latest fad cures and every vitamin remedy on the market. They may prefer health-food stores to doctors' offices. Overweight hypochondriacs have tried every diet available on the Internet and are constantly ready for the next kick to surface. Why? The obsession fires their compulsion.

The same is true for control freaks. They must maintain social order in their own unique fashion whether it's putting dishes in a dishwasher or staying behind the wheel when someone else could just as easily drive. They have an obsession with keeping everybody and every situation under their control. "Hanging out" isn't much of a possibility for controllers. Instead they hang you up!

Getting the feel for how the chart works? The categories help you understand how each compulsive behavior results from an obsession that began with a fear. Our need is to push on and discover the underlying fear that fuels the chain reaction. Without reading further, go back and look at these three examples. Can you sense what the underlying fear might be? Think about it before you read on.

Most of us have a difficult time developing insight into our own areas of need, because we've spent too many years avoiding the fears that invaded our lives. Sometimes facing the bottom line feels so frightening and threatening that we may need help from a counselor to understand what we've kept hidden.

Now that you've had time to reflect, go to the table below and look at what the underlying problem is.

RESULTING COMPULSION	UNDERLYING OBSESSION	UNRESOLVED FEAR
1. Compulsive sexual acts	love	inadequacy
2. Hypochondriacs	health	death
3. Controlling behavior	maintaining order	being abandoned

If you find it difficult to discover the relationship between your fears and obsessions and the compulsions they produce, you're not alone. A counselor's help may be essential. Only after we've struggled to understand how they connect do we develop insight into our issues. In fact, the relationship may not even be based on any actual experience but reside in emotions we have developed about events in the past. The point is: something frightened us, and in time the emotion turned into an obsession that we now express in harmful, repetitious behavior.

THE BOTTOM LINE

Dread of abandonment, inadequacy, or rejection drives the fears of people flying from one person to the next, from counselor to counselor, from friend to friend, from doctor to doctor. And once these people are in a relationship, they desperately cling to the boyfriend or girlfriend out of an inordinate apprehension that the person might disappear. Even though their concerns are overblown, the hidden fear feels like total reality.

Although hypochondriacs may not feel the specter of death has settled into the center of their lives, they cannot live comfortably because of their keen awareness of how quickly human existence can end. These persons may be members of a church emphasizing the eternal security of the believer, but they still are haunted because their theological convictions have never become an emotional reality. Their apprehension translates into a million symptoms of imaginary diseases that still seem quite real to them.

In a completely different manner, controlling spouses may marry passive persons or keep the persons they have married under their thumb. Often they dominate in the workplace and may rise to the top because of the comprehensive grasp they maintain over the entire business. Because they have great success, it's hard to envision them as children cowering in corners, terrified of dominating or even abusive parents.

Nevertheless, their early years of chaos and disorder created a need to keep every aspect of their lives in harmony, lest something blow up and they would again confront disorder and chaos. These individuals may have lived for years in a quiet, relatively passive manner, but when they are threatened, they revert to dominating tendencies. The more out of control people felt as children, the more controlling they tend to become to protect themselves from painful people.

Each of these incidences gives you a feel for how counselors, psychiatrists, and pastoral caregivers observe behavior and then look for the source of problems. We must use a similar process to discover the root system from which our own problems arise.

Now work through this process by analyzing your own behavior. Use this form to get started.

RESULTING COMPULSION	UNDERLYING OBSESSION	UNRESOLVED FEAR
1.		
2.		
3.		

We want to challenge you to consider what you have done here in light of James 1:21, 23–24, a passage that has some important messages about our fears and the compulsions that go along with them.

First, James instructed us to let go of all that is not good and healthy: "Putting aside all filthiness and all that remains of wickedness, in humility receive the word implanted, which is able to save your souls."

Then, he warned us to be active in our obedience to God's Word: "For if anyone is a hearer of the word and not a doer, he is like a man who looks at his natural face in a mirror; for once he has looked at himself and gone away, he has immediately forgotten what kind of person he was." For those of us who are studying our compulsions and fears, this means to be thoughtful—to look deeply and let what we find change us.

We are hopeful that new assignments will lead to new actions—actions away from fear and toward a faith that frees you to become all that God has planned for you to be.

Six

Getting to the Root

Richard Nixon is one of history's most fascinating figures. An intelligent political individual in Washington circles, Nixon was often perceived as having a dark side that eventually led to his downfall during the Watergate period. As the investigation unfolded, one of the most intriguing pieces of data surfaced: the White House tapes!

How could a politically astute person like Richard Nixon allow daily taping of his private conversations and not realize they could discredit him as a leader and finally bring down his presidency? Many psychologically sensitive observers feel the debacle was not an accident. As Robert Wise and Paul Meier reflected on the problem, Paul saw parallels with his own need to fail.

Richard Nixon, like Paul Meier, grew up in a strict religiously legalistic home where maintaining rules proved to be essential. Paul easily envisioned the process that caused Nixon unconsciously to set himself up to fail in the Watergate scandal. The issue? The fear of succeeding!

A Look at Underlying Fear

We've been learning how similar fears subvert our best intentions. The chart in the last chapter traced compulsions backward to discover the fear hiding behind the behavior. Now we'll reverse the procedure and start with fear, observing how it creates the obsessions that push repetitive behaviors.

The problem begins with experiences or feelings we can't face. Sometimes the terror or shame is so great we can't allow ourselves to look clearly and fully at what occurred. Instead, we sweep the event into the back of our memories, hoping the entire experience will disappear. However, like mushrooms, fears grow in the dark, taking shapes and forms we no longer recognize. In fact, we may completely lose our memory of the association between the earlier event and our current behavior. Nevertheless, fear is like fire underneath a steam engine. It's the heat that drives the machine!

In this chapter, we are going to look further at another aspect of our fears. Like runaway fires, these emotional explosions can jump over the tree and send an inferno raging down the valley. Consequently, it's vitally important we understand the nature of the blaze.

Let's look at three of our most poignant emotional fears.

The Fear of Failing

No one wants to fail, but for some people just the possibility is terrifying. We've spoken of Paul Meier's experience with this, and Robert Wise confronted it as well. As a child, Robert was adopted into a family that had struggled to survive the Great Depression. His father carried an obsessive fear that economic disaster would return and cripple America. He saw the stock market as the ultimate source of evil, to be avoided at all cost. While a bright man, Lawrence Wise conducted his business under a cloak of fear, making decisions based on apprehension rather than good business sense. The rub-off on Robert was the constant fear that the country's economy might collapse at any time. Subsequently, during one of the most prosperous decades in American history, Robert went to college believing he should graduate with two complete careers lined up just in case! Careful planning? No, the problem was a fear of failure.

What might a dread of failure produce? For many people the result is an obsession with making money. Often they try to accumulate such a large cash reserve they will never have to worry. Yet, like Ebenezer Scrooge, who was abandoned as a child, they end up working as if all the banks will close tomorrow morning. The fact that these people put making money ahead of personal relationships produces their compulsion.

When the problem becomes severe and obvious, we generally stick a label on their foreheads: *workaholics!* These persons are obsessed with their work and place performance ahead of all relationships. They may have moments when loneliness and emptiness touch them, but they push their true feelings aside with long days of hard work.

The chain reaction? Fear of failing + obsession with money = workaholism.

THE FEAR OF INSIGNIFICANCE

Similar to the fear of failure, thinking we are nobody is equally demeaning. People who struggle with this may feel they don't have the ability to reach high enough even to fail. During their school years, strugglers usually feel no one cares about them and there is no place for them on the social scale. They see themselves as nonachievers, even though they have made significant accomplishments.

When young people feel they don't matter, they are particularly open to four possible obsessions and may get hooked on one, two, three, or all of the drives. One of the easiest snags is the sex hook. As their bodies mature, kids find it easy to start using sex as a way of feeling significant. Waiting in the wings is the world of pornography.

A second temptation confronting seemingly insignificant persons is the quest for power. They easily find themselves pulled toward some expression of social power as a means of obtaining personal value. Adolf Hitler's life will forever be a monument to what can happen when a person who looks like, feels like, and acts like a nobody, sets out to gain personal worth through the exercise of political power. A frightening monument, indeed!

Money and materialism are also a natural allurement. If enough symbols of value can be accumulated, then people who feel they are insignificant can point to their ownership of "stuff" to demonstrate they are truly important. They find a way out of the hole they think they live in by packing home a large income.

Interestingly enough, the Bible speaks about these three attractions as an important proof of sin. "For all that is in the world, the lust of the flesh and the lust of the eyes and the boastful pride of life, is not from the Father but is from the world" (1 John 2:16). The apostle John warned of the danger of loving these three ingredients in the world system: illicit sexuality, personal pride or power, and materialism. These three obsessions reflect the very passions God warns us to avoid.

The fourth danger for people with problems of insignificance is drugs. The emotional and physical high they acquire from a stimulating substance propels people of low self-esteem to feel as if they are sitting on top of the world. Drugs offer the most frightening alternative possible: they can kill their users while killing their pain of feeling insignificant.

These obsessions quickly turn into compulsive behaviors. While we may not think of adults with political power or religious preeminence as being compulsive, they may be working hard to stay on top of their dread of being plunged back into a state of nothingness. Although many bodybuilders and weight lifters train because of their convictions about the importance of health and exercise, extreme muscle types may be flexing their bulging arms to manipulate the opposite sex. As children, they often felt powerless to deal with the overwhelming influence of the parent of the opposite sex. Boys who grew up with absent fathers may attract multiple homosexual lovers to lessen the pain of an unconscious "missing father" addiction.

The chain reaction? Fear of being a nothing + obsessive expressions of lust or power or use of money or drugs = compulsive big-time loser!

THE FEAR OF REJECTION

Parents are of supreme importance to all of us as children. We desperately need our parents' love and want to know we mean the world to Mom *and* Dad. When unconditional love isn't possible, the door opens to a deeply unsettling fear our parents may be about to jettison us out of their lives. Such fear of rejection is terrifying!

As we've seen, the easiest response is to develop a compulsive desire to please the nonaccepting parent. Often workaholics push themselves to achieve in a business that would particularly impress the parent they fear might reject them. The parents may have no idea why their child is such a hard worker, but their expressions of approval encourage the workaholic to keep excelling at an ever-expanding rate.

Another response to fear of rejection is to fail. These children give up and rebel. In order to negate their fears of abandonment, these individuals intend to disappoint the rejecting parent, sometimes consciously and sometimes unconsciously. Often the results are tragic.

We have seen the problem with an overachieving pastor who never seemed to have time for his daughter. The child tried in every way possible to get her father's attention but he didn't warm up to her. As the years went by the daughter rebelled against his biblical values and became a "raving liberal," rejecting the viewpoint her father spent all his time espousing.

Another example is the hostile father who pushed his son into an MBA college program, determined that the young man would succeed in business administration. Finally, the student completed his entire program, except for one five-page term paper. Tragically, the son never finished the assignment and didn't obtain a diploma. His reaction kept him out of a career his father had selected for him.

A third obsessive response to fear of rejection is to seek a substitute for the rejecting parent. Although the replacement may seem to fit the bill for meeting emotional needs, the selection process creates a compulsive behavior that can create lifelong problems. This person may develop a "broken people-picker" tendency, resulting in many painful relationships that mirror the parent-child relationship.

Have you read about a movie star going through her fifth

divorce at age thirty-five? Sadly, the queen of the screen had been married to a long line of sexually abusive men who were not only unfaithful but also addicted to alcohol and drugs. Behind the scenes of this chaotic and fragmented life lay the shadow of a father who had not loved and affirmed his daughter. When Dr. Meier treated this woman in a hospital setting, he discovered the father had been a sexually abusive and alcoholic man. With no insight into her behavior, the movie diva kept trying to fix Dad over and over, over and over, over and over again. She had severe codependency issues. Fortunately, the movie star broke her compulsive "jerk addiction" cycle and recovered from her chronic depression and anxiety disorder.

The chain reaction? Fear of rejection + obsession to please or to disappoint or to substitute = unexpected disaster!

DIGGING UP THE ROOT SYSTEM

The compulsive behaviors in our lives grow out of a fertile garden nourished by the underlying fears from our childhood. The better we understand how those fears were formed and grew, the more capable we will be of getting the weeds out of our lives, a kind of "existential despair." Here's the form we used in the last chapter but reversed to help you consider how your fears produce corresponding behavior. See if yours fit this pattern.

RESULTING COMPULSION	UNDERLYING OBSESSION	UNRESOLVED FEAR
1.		
2.		
3.		

Perhaps you've come to a fresh insight into how the emotional patterns in your life work. Great! That's the objective. If not, close the book for a while and spend time digging in your mental garden until you know what's operating below the surface.

You are not alone in your fears! Psalm 34:4 reveals that David was a fearful man. He wrote, "I sought the LORD, and He answered me, /And delivered me from all my fears." While that verse might frustrate you because you have not been delivered, don't be discouraged. David did not say he was *instantly* delivered from his fears. At this moment, your deliverance is on its way as you seek God and His truth. You are walking the path toward healing and restoration—and you are not alone.

SEVEN

Trouble in Your Backyard

In the past several chapters, we have been considering how your early experiences of fear shape your present behavior. The goal has been to put you in touch with your needs and to help you find answers. But there's more to the story.

Not all our fears come from childhood experiences!

Every morning the sun rises on a world struggling to avoid disasters. Open any morning's newspaper and take a quick scan of the headlines. Troops are in action overseas. A new epidemic is killing a population. Homeland security remains a priority as we try to be prepared to handle any attack against the United States. Income is down so the state is behind on tax collection. Taxes will have to be raised. Agencies will have to cut spending. Republicans yell at Democrats; Democrats accuse Republicans. Tax reforms are promised. Tax reforms don't happen. The repetitious stories go on and on, day after day without end.

We live in a world filled with tension. Often the struggles in the marketplace slip through our front gate and sweep into our backyards. Even though the issues don't directly touch us, the problems have a way of boring into our thoughts and feelings, making us feel as if we are supposed to be out there in a battle that doesn't even belong to us. We need help sorting out these social aberrations.

CONTEMPORARY CULTURAL COLLISIONS

The serious side of this problem surfaces when innocent people get killed walking down the street as an explosion erupts. In the September 11 disasters, many of the victims had simply gone to work or boarded an airplane, expecting nothing more than a typical workday. Suddenly the freedom and openness of American society exploded into a million pieces. Buildings tumbled to the ground! Innocent lives disappeared in an instant!

How can we face the strain of living in such turbulent times? What can describe the feeling of walking through a metal detector at the airport, not knowing if the man in front of us will turn out to be a terrorist? Many contemporary writers, German existential philosophers, artists, and counselors have found a word that seems to best describe the gloomy sense of anxiety or depression arising from these difficult social conditions: *angst*.

Particularly common in the modern world, this sense of undefined fear arises out of *us* more than from anything out of the distant past. It comes with the tenuousness of the modern world, appearing like a dark cloud and settling around us. We dread "something" but can't exactly grasp what it is. Angst is a general, internal, and personal fear that seems to come out of nowhere. Yet, the very real fear can invade and corrupt every area of our lives.

Often this internalized dread arrives when we are by ourselves.

On a nice, warm afternoon, we might be driving down the street with our minds in neutral. Out of nowhere worry bubbles up, and we find ourselves with a growing, gnawing sensation that something is amiss.

On the other hand, we could be in a relaxed posture on a vacation. The sun is slowly sinking as we sail on the cruise ship, drifting through the Caribbean. Or we might be gliding on skis through the Rocky Mountains with gorgeous scenery on every side when we no longer feel good about the sunset or the pines. What's ruining this picture?

Four aspects of our lives in the twenty-first century might create this fear.

First, *the anonymous character of contemporary life* feeds our feelings of angst. A few of us still live on farms and in small enough towns to know virtually everybody in the village, but most of us come from metropolises where we don't even know the name of our next-door neighbor. We drive down four- or six-lane highways with our windows rolled up, in complete segregation from all the other cars filled with people we will never see again.

Although we are not paranoid, the isolation of the moment causes us to feel we may be at risk from strangers lurking in every setting, from a long grocery store line to a local restaurant. When we knew these faces were our friends, we could be comfortable, but now we are not sure if they are good folks or car thieves or terrorists.

The pace of life is another problem. Timesaving gadgets surround us. Thus we move ever faster, at such a constant and rapid pace that we don't have time to reflect on what is occurring around and within us. Because a thoughtful examination of our life situation seldom occurs, we tend to go from mistake to mistake.

When people don't practice the art of reflection and meditation, they slide toward manipulation and practice devious means of affecting the people around them. In time, they turn into a cog in a machine rather than a genuinely warm, caring person.

The foregoing are important factors in the contemporary feeling of angst, but we haven't yet reached the cause that particularly makes this a modern problem. *The loss of divinity* particularly causes angst.

Our age is decidedly different from the past, because our society generally functions as if we have jettisoned God out of the human equation. No prayers at school. No mention of God in the movies or the arts. People often use the name of God as profanity. On and on the list of absences and abuses goes until we end up with the current philosophical view that in the beginning God didn't create heaven and earth; we created God.

If God is gone, what's left? Only me. Lonely, individual, singular, incapable *me*. People without God turn to "me" as their source of hope. Inordinate self-centeredness causes "me" to agonize over my inability to control everything happening in the world. In addition, my own loneliness in a world that has become as void as the vacuum in a lightbulb haunts and negates me. *Existential emptiness* ultimately produces angst.

When we lose God, we have lost everything.

GOING UP OR GOING DOWN?

Recently, Robert Wise was waiting for his flight to return to Oklahoma City. Poised at the gate, he was ready to leap across the line the moment the boarding started. The announcement came, but then a man walked up behind Robert and asked him to step to one side. He had been randomly selected for an extensive second search before boarding the commuter airplane.

Knowing he had no choice, Robert put on the most casual smile he could muster and allowed the intensive search of everything he was carrying. Slowly and with painstaking accuracy, the security agent went through every inch of Robert's briefcase and a sack in which he carried a computer and materials for the book he was writing. Then the agent traced up and down and across Robert's body with a metal detector. The search ended about the same time as the last passengers boarded the airplane. With a grim look on his face, Robert entered the craft and started looking for space where he might store his carry-ons. Most of the overhead bins were packed.

Robert dropped into his seat, feeling rather shaken. After jockeying for quick entry and ample time to stow his goods, he ended up in exactly the position he'd been trying to avoid. The airplane started down the runway but angst had already contaminated his best thoughts. Robert wasn't sure why, but the search left him feeling anxious. The plane was going up, but his feelings were going down! What could he do? Here are some suggestions for handling similar nebulous feelings.

GESTALT "GO-GETTERS"

Originally developed in Germany by psychologist Max Weitheimer (1880–1943) and popularized in America by German-born psychiatrist Fritz Perls (1893–1970), Gestalt psychology takes a new approach to understanding human behavior. Rather than analyzing and dividing people's responses into many parts (like what we felt in our childhood, our adolescence, or our adult years), this dynamic system suggests we are a whole, and the best way to affect change is by dealing with our total behavior at this moment.

In Gestalt group therapy, body language is as important as verbal communication. Clients are urged to be honest, to think out loud as they express their feelings. The group members respond to each other's mood changes in a forthright manner. Often clients get in touch with feelings they have never expressed before. Dreams are also analyzed. This system, even when practiced alone, can offer help for our culturally conditioned fears.

The following exercise puts Gestalt thought to work, using Robert Wise's experience on the airplane as an example. How might Robert have dealt with the angst he felt when he didn't have a place to store his gear after the agent searched him so extensively? What was *really* bothering him?

Step One: Use Your Imagination

Our wonderful sense of imagination can open the door to our unconscious side and allow thoughts and feelings to come together in new harmony. We need to allow our creative imaginations to help us get inside our feelings of angst in a new and insightful manner. Let's try it.

Robert is sitting in his seat, looking out of the airplane as it rolls down the runway to take off. He doesn't like the irritation he is feeling. He makes a conscious decision to let his imagination help him solve the problem.

Step Two: Cancel Self-Censorship

In this step, we make a conscious decision to allow full exploration of the "something" bothering us, regardless of where the probing takes us. We shut off all judgments for the moment.

Robert consciously decides to explore his feelings regardless of what might surface. He stops judging himself and allows whatever is working behind the scenes to come forth.

Step Three: Start a Conversation with Yourself

We need to give our imaginations full reign and pretend our alter ego is sitting next to us. Whatever comes from our subconscious is fine.

Robert begins by pulling out a sheet of blank paper and starting a conversation, just as he does when he is writing dialogue in a novel. He allows his imagination to guide the discussion in the emotion-filled talkfest he's writing out.

"Hello," he writes. "Alter ego, I need your help in sorting out why this lengthy search at the terminal gate bothered me so much."

"Okay," his imagination responds. "I'm willing to try to see if we can come up with anything."

"I positioned myself to get on this airplane first and then this jerk nailed me because my name came up in a random search. It really is disconcerting."

"I think the terrorist events and being grabbed for a search are more emotional than you have admitted to yourself."

Robert thinks for a moment and then writes slowly, "I suppose so. I fly so often I don't like to think about the possibility of an attack happening on any airplane I'm riding on. The thought's unnerving."

"Then," Robert's imagination responds, "having such a complete and totally thorough search actually did bother you?"

"More than I'd like to admit," Robert writes, "but I'm so familiar with these searches I hate to think that one unnerved me."

"But it did," the alter ego answers. "You have to face the fact."

Step Four: Let Insight Emerge

For a moment Robert stares at the piece of paper. "What am I going to do with this feeling?"

"Hey," Robert's imagination answers immediately, "you've focused on the wrong issue. You were carefully searched to make sure the airplane is totally secure. The examination means you're on a completely safe airplane. Instead of being anxious, you ought to feel exhilarated."

The process ends here. Robert has his answer. The "something" is clarified. He can see it is possible to relax.

Building a Sound Foundation

God's plan has never been for His people to live in fear. To the contrary, the Bible tells us that our heavenly Father has given us a spirit of power, love, and self-control (2 Tim. 1:7). Loving God sets us free from loving this world too much. The answer to angst is adoration! Praising, blessing, loving, and thanking God shifts our preoccupation with ourselves. Worship reorients our perspective, and we get in emotional touch with the fact that God truly runs this world—and we can fear less for life.

Now let's practice the Gestalt approach. Can you get in touch with any experience of angst in your own life? Remember a moment when nagging worry settled in for no good reason? Maybe a quick prayer for insight and guidance would help. If "something" appears, go back and get in touch with the situation. Use the space below to start working on the issue.

Step One: Use Your Imagination

_____ Yes! I will allow my imagination to work on this problem.

Step Two: Cancel Self-Censorship

_____ Yes! The exploration can take me wherever I need to go. I won't censor my thoughts or emotions.

Step Three: Start a Conversation with Yourself

_____ Yes! I will talk to myself, using a piece of paper or the space below to start the conversation. I will also talk to any people from my past or present who come to mind by imagining those individuals sitting across from me.

Step Four: Let Insight Emerge

_____ Yes! I have insight. It is:

EIGHT

Not-So-Fascinating Phobias

The Bible provides us with God's truth and wisdom. Some Christians say that if we only tried harder to memorize biblical truth, our problems would vanish. The implication is that we don't need to look inward, we simply need to look upward. If we get enough truth in our heads, we will heal whatever hurts hide in our souls.

We do need truth, but we also need to look within ourselves to discover where and how best to apply that truth. Lamentations 3:40 says, "Let us examine and probe our ways." Let's continue the search. A look at Marjorie's situation can help.

Marjorie couldn't remember when her button problem started. At some indefinable time she began to have a fear of those shiny little fasteners holding her clothes together—particularly when they lay harmlessly in another person's hand. At first, the sight of a button in someone else's hand created just a slight sense of dread within Marjorie, but with time the feeling increased and her anxiety became more pronounced. Finally, anyone opening his palm and revealing a button would send Marjorie into a panic attack. While no good reason for the overwhelming fear seemed to exist, Marjorie had a phobia of buttons.

As is true of angst, phobias may be difficult to trace to their origins. Probably some situation or experience created a sense of urgency, and that's where the problem started. But many times a therapist cannot find the root cause. Phobias simply may feel as if they floated in through our bedroom window and grabbed us! Consequently, the source isn't the issue with this problem.

Meet Alicia

Alicia Randolph spent thirty years of her life locked inside her small home because she was terrified of leaving the apartment. Alicia had grown up in Newark, New Jersey, with the city and surrounding area always feeling familiar. Yet some unnoted past experience had bothered her.

The phobia began far back in the early 1950s, long before anyone had heard of Legionnaires' disease, the Boston Strangler, The Godfather, or Osama bin Laden. When the problem started, nothing in the newspapers would have frightened Alicia. However, during the ensuing three decades, she left her apartment only twice. Once she went out for a family funeral, and another time Alicia was forced to go to a local hospital for medical care, but she immediately returned and locked the door tightly behind her. Why? No reason ever surfaced—except a nameless fear.

Alicia Randolph probably would have eventually been found dead in the apartment she hid in day after day, year after year, if a psychologist had not moved in next door. Eventually, therapist

George Duke noticed the recluse and began to explore her strange behavior. In time, George was able to coax Alicia into seeking help, which started to break the chains of her phobia. With therapy, she worked free of her dread of living in a normal social environment.

Alicia had developed agoraphobia, a fear of being in open and public places. As strange as her problem sounds, a survey by the National Institute of Mental Health reported that roughly one adult in twenty suffers from a phobia similar to Alicia's.[1] While they may have no idea how the phobia developed, these "phobics" became captives of their phobias.

A Vast Array of "What-Ifs"

The director of Washington's Center of Behavioral Medicine called phobias "the malignant disease of the 'what-if's,' the exponential growth of imaginary disasters that can choke rational thought."[2] And that's the problem! The capacity of a long-held dread to emerge from insignificance and grow so large it keeps us from thinking intelligently makes phobias difficult to face. Like the effect of angst, the contamination of our rationality keeps us from enjoying life in a full and meaningful way.

Any official list of phobias will be vast, running from acrophobia (the fear of heights) to xenophobia (the fear of strangers). In the appendix, we have listed 205 of the most common phobias. You may be surprised to discover that people can develop compulsive fears of everything from darkness to dolls to dust. If nothing else, the list makes fascinating reading. On the other hand, you may discover your own particular apprehension described in that list or the following short one, which mentions the most common fears people encounter on a daily basis.

acrophobia: heights

ailurophobia: cats

anthropophobia: people

arachnaphobia: spiders

autophobia: aloneness

claustrophobia: closed spaces

gephyrophobia: bridges

mikrophobia: germs

nyctophobia: darkness

aerophobia: flying

amaxophobia: driving

aquaphobia: water

astraphobia: lightning

brontophobia: thunder

cynophobia: dogs

herpetophobia: reptiles

murophobia: mice

Our most common phobias arise from a fear of physical danger or personal injury. For example, Dr. Meier has seen many patients over the years who have general phobias, such as the fear of flying, driving, crossing bridges, riding elevators, and standing in high places.[3] Each one shares the trait of fear of an object or a situation. A quick survey of the wide range of phobias demonstrates that it's possible to develop an obsessive fear of almost anything.

WHAT IS A PHOBIA?

Phobias are obsessive, compulsive, constant fears that remain one of the most powerful forces in the human psyche. Born out of the concern for self-protection, a phobia raises our apprehensions about survival to the ultimate level of self-preoccupation. Even though the fulfillment of most of our phobias demands that we negate what logic tells us can't be denied, the fear still "feels" rational—even when we know it is irrational.

One of the strange dimensions of this fearful intrusion is that people with phobias already recognize the absurdity of their situation. While people who are paranoid believe there is a basis for their apprehension, phobics know this isn't the case—but it doesn't make any difference. The obsessive fear continues. Even though it's irrational, the people with a phobia don't imagine they are afraid, they *truly are* afraid!

But wait! There's good news ahead.

While the origin of a phobia may be difficult to identify and the effects of the fear can prove overwhelming, phobias are one of the most curable emotional problems. A wide variety of therapeutic techniques can help phobics find relief.

WHAT CAN WE DO?

Some estimates for the number of agoraphobia sufferers in this country run as high as twenty million people. Let's take another look at the problem of agoraphobia and see what clues we can pick up for dealing with the phobia.

Although Mary Brown had a good marital relationship for twenty years, she avoided going to restaurants with her husband. She preferred to stay in the house. Often when sitting in a public place like church or a basketball game, Mary would be gripped by fear. She wanted to stand up and scream, "Somebody call an ambulance! I'm suffocating. Help me!"

Mary's first attack occurred during her teenage years. As the years went by, her dread of crowds grew, and by the time she reached college she did everything she could to stay out of packed areas such as football games. On some occasions, she would break out in hot and cold flashes. Her heart would start to pound and Mary quickly felt dizzy. As her panic grew worse, she would shake. But most difficult of all were the moments when everything around her took on the feeling of unreality. The world seemed to be getting smaller and smaller. Mary Brown's entire life seemed to be shrinking to an intolerable size.

Unfortunately, Mary's world is typical for agoraphobics. For unexplained reasons, the overwhelming majority of agoraphobics are women. Men tend to deal with their anxiety by becoming alcoholics. Role stereotyping makes it easier for women to stay at home. While they may not be in touch with the problem, their first panic attack probably arose from some form of stress.

SEEKING HELP

You may be surprised to learn that early in the Bible is an important story about one of the first phobias noted in literature. Because this man's greatness remained so vast, we don't usually explore his emotional needs but he did have a significant problem.

Turn to Exodus 3, and you'll read the story of the Lord confronting Moses with the task of returning to Egypt to challenge the pharaoh. The earlier chapters reveal a picture of a normal, emotionally healthy man, but as this chapter opens we discover Moses had a phobia about speaking in public. All the classic symptoms are there. While Moses could act with considerable boldness, speaking brought him to his knees because of his phobic reaction.

This man of God had a mission paramount to Israel's future and ultimately the Lord's intentions for the entire world. Moses surely needed the miraculous gifts God gave him for the task. He could turn his rod into a snake or make his hand become leprous. In addition, Moses was empowered to turn the waters of the Nile into blood. If God would so endow this Jewish leader, why wouldn't He instantly cure him of the phobia? The Bible doesn't answer our question but tells us God instructed

Moses to use his brother, Aaron, as his spokesman. In other words, Moses was left to confront his psychological problem in much the same way we are! And that's what causes us to grow.

Reading between the lines, we can pick up some important clues from the story of Moses for how we can find help in dealing with phobias. Here are three specific ways you can start bringing change.

1. Recognize You're Not Alone

Moses had to recognize that he wasn't by himself up there on the mountain when God spoke through the burning bush. His first step was to recognize that God walked with him. At every moment of his life, the Creator of the universe stood by Moses—and if you are His, He stands beside you as well.

Feel like a freak in a normal world? It isn't true. The world is filled with millions of people struggling with exactly the same fears. Learning to feel "normal" about a behavior issue will help to break us loose from these chains that bind us.

Many people seek out support groups that allow them to talk about their fears with a larger framework of friends who share the same phobias. These friends can call each other when they feel their phobias gaining control. Such emotional support lifts strugglers to a new level of competency.

The most important discovery is that God has always been with us during this conflict. We need to call on Him to help us keep from thinking we're all alone in a huge, unconcerned world.

2. Enlist Your Family

Understanding and bolstering from our family members makes a world of difference. We need to be honest and straightforward about our fears. Their help may be needed in getting us involved with professional care. More important, we need to be able to talk with someone close at hand about what we're feeling. Having the people we care about listen with openness and compassion can give us emotional strength to face our phobias.

Quite possibly Moses had difficulties going to his brother, Aaron, and asking for his help in facing such a formidable adversary as the pharaoh. Moses may even have struggled to admit out loud that he had a phobia. Nevertheless, God's answer for Moses was that he seek the help of his brother.

Get honest with your family!

3. Consult the Professionals

If we need insight, input, and direction to find our way out of the maze of our phobias, we can turn to a counseling professional with special skills in this area. We've come a long way from the world of Moses, 1,450 years before Christ. Today, psychiatrists, psychologists, counselors, and pastoral caregivers are trained to help people with these concerns. Unfortunately, many people wait so long to seek professional help, their phobias only grow in size and impact.

Another aspect of this step involves accepting that treatment costs money. We have known those whose churches have supported them and others who've raised the money in a variety of ways. Whatever the source of payment, treatment is worth it. No one should spend his life struggling with overwhelming fear and anxiety attacks. Make a decision right now that you are willing to pay the cost.

Usually counseling is short-term, lasting from three to twelve months. During this time, the counselors can take you through the steps modifying your behavior and giving you insight into the problem. In some cases, medications or additional private sessions with a counselor are needed. Remember, as terrible as phobias feel, they are the most curable of all emotional problems!

Ephesians 5:13 says, "Everything exposed by the light becomes visible" (NIV). It is important for us to be willing to allow God's light to shine on our lives and make known those things hidden in darkness. Psychological treatment shines a light on those unknown areas that are causing you to be paralyzed by fear or at least dead to what God has for you.

Ephesians 5:14 goes on to provide a rallying cry for all who are stuck in fear: "Wake up, O sleeper,/ rise from the dead,/ and Christ will shine on you" (NIV). So whatever is holding you back, whatever excuse has kept you dead in fear, rise and wake up to a world of people who want to help you experience the freedom that can be found when fear is resolved.

In the next chapter, we will consider some specific exercises and techniques used to reduce or eliminate the problems phobias may have created in the past. You will discover instruction in how to turn panic attacks, which can come from phobias or other sources like past experiences or genuinely dangerous circumstances, into personal achievement!

NINE

Stop the Attack

Stephen Arterburn lives in Laguna Beach on southern California's shoreline. Not far behind his offices are the towering slopes of Saddleback Mountain. The land of perpetual spring always provides tourists with the beauty of the sea and the mountains' heights. Recently, friends came from Pennsylvania for a visit, and Stephen and his wife drove the couple, Jack and Betty French, up the dirt road running to the peak of Saddleback.

Near the top of the high mountain terrain, Steve and his wife stopped, so they could all get out and stand on a ledge to look out over the valley below them. They assumed Jack and Betty would find the sheer drop down the side of the cliff to be an exhilarating view. As they walked to the edge, Stephen noticed Betty trailing behind them.

"Hey, catch up and look at this plunging drop," Stephen said. "The view will thrill you."

"I— I— I— think not," Betty stammered.

"You'll love it," Stephen replied.

"No . . . no." Betty started walking backward. "Heights bother me."

Jack French had already walked to the edge of the cliff and stopped. "Don't come any closer," he yelled to his wife. "This is no place for you."

Stephen noticed that Betty had begun to breathe harder and a red blotch appeared on her neck.

"Heights bother me," she could barely explain as she kept inching away. "I—I—don't think I can breathe."

Jack ran toward his wife. "Sit down," he demanded. "Sit down, Betty! Look the other way!"

Stephen instantly realized Betty was an acrophobic and a panic attack had hit.

What Is a Panic Attack?

A panic attack is a sudden, unexpected explosion of emotions, striking without apparent cause. Usually a panic attack peaks around ten minutes after it starts and results in symptoms like heart palpitations, sweating, trembling, hyperventilation, nausea, dizziness, chest pains, chills or hot flashes, and numbness. Worst of all, sufferers feel they are going crazy or dying. All personal control seems to have vanished.

These encounters trip the flight-or-fight psychological system, which doesn't make distinctions between what is and is not appropriate. When the internal wiring system popularly called "nerves" flips, the impulses cause human bodies to respond as if a lion has jumped out of the refrigerator. Even though the basement is empty, the physiological system acts as if it's filled with Osama bin Laden's terrorists, rushing upstairs to attack *you!*

Often a phobia will be behind the panic mechanism, setting off an attack. For example, agoraphobia, the fear of being in some-place where escape is difficult, can start fear attacks. The dread of being in a crowd, or on a bridge, or traveling by a bus or a train can release the distress mechanism. As a phobic approaches these situations, the heart starts beating faster and the physical system spins out of control.

What pulls the trigger, releasing this barrage of physical pain? Actually, the answer isn't entirely clear. Some people develop panic attacks; some don't. Panic attacks rarely start in people more than forty-five years old; the first ones usually occur between late adolescence and the mid-thirties. We do know that some panic attacks are completely unrelated to phobias. A wide range of circumstances can cause these attacks, from fearful childhood experiences that we remember when something similar occurs in present-day events, like a packed room or a snake in the backyard.

Let's start with how you can face a specific phobia. Because phobias and panic attacks are related, common solutions will help us deal with both of them.

FEARS THAT BITE

Norman Sparks had been a successful pastor for ten years. While he usually started speaking in a halting manner, by the time he got to the end of his sermons, he had always challenged his congregation with a powerful message. No one suspected that Norman had a significant speaking phobia, but he eventually came to see Dr. Paul Meier.

"Members of my church would not believe I'm here." Norman sounded embarrassed. "But every time I preach I develop severe problems. I start breathing hard and will even shake," Norman admitted. "Maybe I'm in the wrong calling."

Paul watched fear crowd into Norman's eyes. "Norman," he said sympathetically, "you'd be amazed to know how many pastors visit us at our New Life Clinics. They have exactly the same problem you do."

Norman's eyes widened. "You are kidding!"

"Not at all. Many pastors struggle to keep anxieties from completely shutting them down. We can help you deal with your problem."

Norman was quite relieved to hear Dr. Meier's response. He had expected a pronouncement that he was incurable and ought to change professions. Not so! In fact, Paul suggested an approach you can use to help stop the emotional avalanches created by phobias and panic attacks.

Technique One: Desensitization

Regardless of where and why a phobia started, with time the compulsive fear grows into the size of the Japanese Air Force attacking Pearl Harbor. We become supersensitive to the problem.

Our first need is to reduce the aura that has built up around the initial fear. Should anyone be afraid of speaking to a large group of people? Sure. Should anyone be afraid of being afraid? No. That's the issue that needs desensitization.

What could Norman do? Paul suggested he begin by practicing his sermons in front of a few other people before he stood up on Sunday morning. Perhaps speaking to an associate pastor, a youth minister, or a secretary would be a good starting point. Or Norman might ask his wife and children to listen with the understanding that they were helping him face a problem (and then possibly go home after Sunday school so they don't have to listen to his sermon twice!).

Asking for help can be an important part of the desensitization process. While this is not always the case, many times people with specific phobias are perfectionistic. Trying to do everything at impossibly high standards, they set themselves up for overload and panic attacks follow. They need to talk with other people about these secret fears.

We suggest five steps to successfully work through the desensitization process:

1. Openly and Honestly Confront the Problem

Despite Robert Wise's childhood adventures in mountain climbing, in adulthood he unexpectedly discovered a fear of heights. When this problem emerged, Robert was baffled. One of the childhood pranks he and his friends played had been jumping across the open space between buildings three or four-stories high. In fact, he had dived off the highest diving board at the local swimming pool when he was a child.

And as an adult Robert enjoyed flying, never fearing the take-off or landing. Yet, walking across an open three-story-high bridge into an auditorium proved to be a source of apprehension that produced an increased heart rate and wobbly steps. Every time he attended a concert or was at any other lofty location where he was required to look down, Robert experienced these sensations. The problem needed desensitization.

Even though he hated to admit that it frightened him, Robert decided to face the problem head-on. He would confront the fear in every possible way.

2. Ask for God's Help

Robert prayed about the fear, asking Jesus Christ to help him release it. This prayer involved more than simply telling God that emotional bombers were flying over his fortress. Instead, Robert decided to meditate on his fear. He positioned himself in a place where he couldn't be disturbed. Surrounded by total quiet, Robert slowly prayed until he had come into a complete awareness of the presence of God. Sometimes he could do this quickly but other times, it took much longer. At that point, he would ask God's love to enter his fears and remove the effects of excessive apprehension. Robert might even imagine the hand of Christ reaching inside and lifting fear out of him.

These repeated spiritual exercises brought relief. The fear no longer felt overwhelming; now he felt he could manage it.

3. Put Panic into Context

Panic affects you physically. You can hyperventilate without knowing what happened to you. Your heart starts pounding and your breath comes in quick gasps. In a few moments, it feels as if you are suffocating, which only increases the problem! You need to learn to breathe in a way that will diminish the effects of the attack.

Sometimes called "subtle overbreathing," this technique helps you get your rapid breathing under control. Using your shoulders and chest, you take short, quick breaths. Rather than using your diaphragm, you pump your chest for a rapid intake of air. Such a process of skewed breathing decreases the amount of carbon dioxide in your bloodstream and enables the blood to carry more oxygen. This may sound as if you are re-creating the hyperventilation experience. Yes, you are, but hyperventilation is an internal reaction; spontaneously controlling it is a process that you choose to do. Simply controlling your breathing will do wonders to help bring panic under control.

How can you put your panic moments into context? Have

you possibly failed to recognize what person (like a certain size individual), event (like a terrorist attack), or situation (like an unexpected dog outside your door) might initiate your panic attacks? Identify these triggers in the space below:

4. Share the Problem

James 5:16 says, "Confess your sins to each other and pray for each other so that you may be healed" (NIV). What corrects sin also works for curing fear. We must become willing to share, or at least enter into a conversation about our fears. We need to discuss what bothers us with an honest, caring person so we can allow some sunlight to shine on this dark, closed-in area.

Often, talking starts to open the doors that seem so tightly shut. Robert's best confidante is his wife, Margueritte. He knows that telling her his feelings will bring an honest, intelligent response.

The next time Robert and Margueritte went to the civic center where they had to cross this open three-story-high bridge to enter the theater area, Robert admitted the experience bothered him. He tried to calmly convey that walking across such a wide-open area as he looked down had become a problem.

As a trained therapist, Margueritte immediately picked up on the implications. "You sound fearful," she said kindly.

Robert stared at the three-story drop and tightened his jaw. "Yes."

"Notice I'm standing in the center of the crossway," Margueritte said. "I am safe and not in any jeopardy. You can walk over to me." She beckoned.

"Yes," Robert repeated, taking his eyes off the drop. "I'll keep my attention on you."

Margueritte smiled confidently. "You will do fine."

Robert started across.

His wife's response helped him be more rational about the problem. Desensitization had taken another step forward. Confrontation worked!

5. Defeat the Problem

Remember, even though our phobias may be absurd, we really are afraid. The most effective way to undercut our apprehension is to force ourselves to face the emotion. Robert decided he would return to the civic center and keep walking across the bridge until some aspect of the problem changed. Sound easy? Not to Robert!

Robert went back to the civic center a number of times and walked across the bridge. Each time he felt a significant sense of dread, but he made himself walk slowly, looking determinedly straight ahead. He repeated this process until he felt the problem was more manageable.

Force yourself to be around the problem and accept whatever triggers your fear attacks. This is one of the best ways to stop fear explosions. Desensitization can help you calm frayed nerves and keep your heart from beating like a runaway bass drum. You need to crank up bravery and march forward!

TECHNIQUE TWO: PARADOXICAL INTENTION

During our childhoods, many of us developed a tendency to be defiant. Perhaps some authority figure pushed us too hard and we developed resistance in response. We can actually use this to our advantage in defeating emotional attacks. Here's how a therapist might use paradoxical intention as a tool.

A client came into Dr. Paul Meier's office with a problem of recurrent panic attacks. George was terrified these explosions would erupt at any moment. Paul leaned back in his chair and said, "Okay, make it happen."

The client blinked. "What?"

"Go ahead and do it right now," Paul repeated. "Let's observe what occurs."

Looking stunned, George started to frown. "You mean . . . do it right *here?*"

"Sure. I want to see the panic happen."

The frown deepened. George abruptly realized no matter how great his fear was, he couldn't make the panic attack emerge.

Then Paul went one step further. He suggested, "Whenever a panic attack starts, try to make it worse, George. Can you do that?"

"No, I don't think so."

Paul challenged George to try this in the next week or so. And George did. At those moments his nervous system would actually rebel and make the attack subside. This strange paradox had the power to bring his problem under control.

Paradoxical intention is another form of letting the sunlight shine in a closed space. We are forcing our obsessive behavior to take a walk in the light rather than hide in some dark corner. Then we discover that we have an unexpected control over the situation.

You can practice this same approach to deal with the exploding fears in your life. Recognize that the attacks will do the opposite of what you command. Make paradox work for you!

Paradoxical intention can also be used in many practical ways. When Paul Meier's wife asks him to buy a loaf of bread on the way home from work, Paul is often afraid he'll forget. Therefore, he tries to forget on purpose and is unable to do so.

Try it. You'll be surprised.

Technique Three:
Putting Insight to the Task

Cognitive therapy is a similar approach, helping us make sense out of what feels like an emotional avalanche. This form of psychological insight allows our minds to work more effectively by looking below the surface of our behavior. Again, let's observe how it works in therapy.

Thomas Johnson came to Dr. Paul Meier's office with great apprehension that his next panic attack would drive him over the edge. He sat nervously in the chair with his fingers intertwined, tensely chewing on his lip. "I'm afraid I'm going to slip into insanity if I have another one of these attacks," he explained. "Dr. Meier, I'm afraid I'll go crazy."

Paul listened quietly and then replied, "When you've had these attacks previously, did you ever go crazy?"

Thomas stopped and looked puzzled. "No. No, I didn't go crazy."

"You never went crazy?" Paul repeated. "Did you go crazy yesterday when you had a panic attack?"

"No." Johnson shook his head. "No, I didn't."

"Did you go crazy this morning?"

Johnson kept shaking his head. "No, I've never gone crazy."

"Then why would you go crazy during your next attack?"

Thomas opened his mouth but couldn't say anything.

"Any logical reason I've missed?"

Johnson scratched his head and looked mystified. After several moments of silence, he answered, "No, no there really isn't, but they *could* get worse!"

"Yes, that's possible," Dr. Meier replied. "But I've seen your psychological testing and thoroughly evaluated you myself, and I can vouch for the fact that even though one out of every thirty-three people in the world lose touch with reality periodically, *you* are not going to become one of them."

Insight helps us to recognize we are fearing something that doesn't actually exist. What started out as one problem has multiplied into two forms. The panic attack is one thing, but our interpretation of its meaning is another matter. Cognitive therapy helps us sort out the mix-up and recognize these emotional attacks don't necessarily mean what we may have thought they did.

Dr. Meier had another patient who was convinced she would die in one of her panic attacks. The concern had left the woman in a nearly immobilized state of mind.

"I know I'll die," Maria blurted out.

"How long have you been having these attacks?" Paul asked

"Oh, my goodness!" Maria exclaimed. "For years."

"Ever die from one of them?"

Maria's exasperation turned to scorn. "Of course not!" she snapped. "I'm still here."

"Then, why will the next one kill you?"

Like Thomas Johnson, Maria was stopped in her tracks. She didn't know what to say because her claims were so irrational. Push yourself to consider whether your "fear of your fears" has any basis in fact. You'll find it doesn't!

TECHNIQUE FOUR: WRITE IT DOWN

What if your fears cause you to worry all day long? The truth is, you're like a million other people. Worrying can become like a phobia, popping up when you least need the intrusion. Here's a suggestion for the worriers.

Put a packet of index cards in your pocket or purse and use

these 3 x 5 cards to write down those intruding worries. Set a time later that night when you'll pull out the cards, give yourself thirty minutes, and worry on a time schedule. Just remember that every time one of these concerns appears, you'll write it down and refuse to worry at that moment while promising yourself that you *will* worry about it on purpose at the scheduled time that night.

Here's what will happen. The mere act of making a list and putting your worries on a schedule erases their immediate power. Often when you consider the list, you will end up angry with yourself for even entertaining such nonsense. On the other hand, if the problem has merit, you may be able to face it constructively during your "worry time" and come to important decisions about how to move forward. You get something accomplished.

At the least, you take the energy out of the habit of compulsive worrying. Rather than your concerns controlling you, you are able to control your concerns.

One aspect of controlling panic attacks remains, and that is medication. We'll discuss that in chapter 12. For the time being, analyze how panic attacks can disrupt your life. Using what you've read above, identify the technique you will start using to put these emotions in a harness. And then use the space below to write down a plan to conquer your panic attacks. Remember that while the solutions above seem quite simplistic, in reality each one was surrounded by ongoing counseling, and, in some cases, the insight came while the patient was on medication.

TEN

Nothing Like
a Good Night's Sleep

Joan Clement called Dr. Robert Wise at the church, almost demanding to see him. Joan had had a dream that terrified her. She knew Robert had studied dreams and often spoke about their place in Scripture. A day after her phone call Joan showed up with tears in her eyes.

"I'm panicked," she began in a trembling voice. "I almost can't even talk about my dream."

"Just relax," Robert answered. "Usually our dreams are attempting to give us good news, not bad."

"Oh no!" Joan objected. "This dream is so terrible there couldn't be anything good about it."

"Okay, start at the beginning and share the details with me."

"Two nights ago I dreamed I was coming to church and walked into the sanctuary." Joan almost choked as she struggled to keep speaking. "I looked up and saw a funeral was in progress." Tears began running down her face. "I walked down the aisle and suddenly realized the funeral was for my daughter. Dr. Wise, I'm afraid my little Carla is going to die!"

For a moment Robert considered the situation. He really didn't know Joan or her family but from his work with dreams he had a strong sense of what was happening. "How old is your daughter?"

"Five."

"Did she just start kindergarten?"

"Why, yes. A few weeks ago."

Robert smiled. "As I said earlier, your dream is trying to give you good news. In most dreams, death is a symbol of transformation. This dream is telling you that your relationship with your child is changing radically. You've thought of her as a baby, but the first stage of her life is behind you now. Carla's off to school and is growing up. The dream is calling your attention to the fact that you've got to make adjustments to her recent development."

Joan's mouth dropped. "That's right!" she gasped. "Exactly right! I've been trying to keep her functioning like a baby."

In seconds Joan Clement recognized the truth her dream was pushing her to see. Rather than fear, Joan needed an attitude of expectation and hope. Carla was entering a new phase in her young life, and she and her mom could enjoy that as much as they had her earlier years. In dreams, death isn't necessarily what it appears to be—and that's good news.

DON'T BE AFRAID!

Fears often explode in the night. In this chapter we will explore remedies for dreams that haunt us. Like Ebenezer Scrooge's experience in Charles Dickens's *A Christmas Carol,* ghosts of the past sometimes show up for visits to make us into better people. Because dreams can be so vivid and powerful, people often fear what they've dreamed.

Many Christians assume looking at their dreams is a New Age phenomenon to be avoided at all costs. They need to listen to Abraham Lincoln, who said: "How much there is in the Bible about dreams! There are, I think, some sixteen chapters in the Old Testament and four or five in the New in which dreams are mentioned . . . If we believe in the Bible, we must accept the fact that, in the old days, God and His angels came to humans in their sleep and made themselves known in dreams."[1]

When Robert Wise and Paul Meier were writing *Windows of the Soul,* a book that discusses using dreams for personal spiritual development, they discovered at least 151 direct references to dreams in the Bible. These ranged from Jacob's powerful Old Testament dream of a stairway leading up into heaven to Joseph's New Testament dream to take the baby Jesus and His mother, Mary, and flee to Egypt. The Bible is filled with positive examples of the use of dreams and visions (a dream one sees with one's eyes open) to give guidance and direction. These include: God's direction for Gideon (Judg. 6:14; 7:13–15), His call to Samuel (1 Sam. 3:9–10), His message to Nathan for King David (2 Sam. 12), and Daniel's amazing ability to see the future through dreams (Dan. 1:17). In the New Testament, Matthew's gospel begins with an angel of the Lord speaking to Joseph in a dream and telling him to take Mary as his wife (Matt. 1:20). Peter's radical acceptance of Gentiles into the Christian faith was the result of a dream (Acts 10:9–48). The New Testament ends with John's amazing experience in a vision that resulted in the book of Revelation (Rev. 1:10–11).

The Old Testament tells us that God generally spoke to the prophets in visions and dreams. God communicated differently with Moses by speaking to him directly. In other words, Israel's general expectation was for God to speak through the dream mechanism.

Hear now My words:
If there is a prophet among you,
I, the LORD, shall make Myself known
  to him in a vision.
I shall speak with him in a dream.
Not so, with My servant Moses,
He is faithful in all My household;
With him I speak mouth to mouth,
Even openly, and not in dark sayings,
And he beholds the form of the LORD.
Why then were you not afraid
To speak against My servant, against
  Moses? (Num. 12:6–8)

During the next five centuries the evolving church continued to anticipate God's speech occurring through their dreams. The writings of Justin Martyr, Irenaeus, Origen, Augustine, John Chrysostom, and many other church fathers describe the same experience as in the Old and New Testaments. Superstition first entered the picture with Jerome's translation of the Bible into Latin near the end of the third century. Unfortunately, he mistranslated the word *anan*, which forbids witchcraft or soothsaying, by also including the analyzing of dreams. Because the Latin Vulgate translation gained such comprehensive status in the succeeding centuries, his mistake cast a shadow over the practice of interpreting dreams.

Yet Jerome rejected the writings of the Greek classics and became a monk entirely because of a dream. The experience of dreaming remained a major ingredient in Jerome's ministry.[2] Today we have returned to the same perspective observed in the Bible. Even though they may sometimes frighten us, dreams are still one of God's ways to communicate with us. We don't have to be apprehensive.

WHAT IS A DREAM?

Many dreams are symbolic statements. Rather than using the colloquial speech of everyday language, dreams are more like the movies, telling us a story that has the power to change how we feel and think. "We" are the movie producer, the actors, the objects like a car or house in the dream, as well as the story line. Virtually every aspect of the story is about us.

To better understand our dreams, we need to shift gears out of our rational minds and look at the symbolic language of dreams and how it can reveal truth in unique ways. Here are some questions that can help you begin to understand the symbolic expressions of your dreams. Ask yourself how your dream symbols fit these inquiries:

- Where have I seen this entity in my dream before?
- What did this object mean to me in the past?
- What does the dream figure mean to me right now?
- What meaning does it embody?

For example, let's say that last night you dreamed a tattoo had appeared on your shoulder. And let's assume you have always disliked tattoos and the idea of one on your shoulder is offensive. You didn't like this tattoo of a woman who looked amazingly like the well-known movie star and singer Cher. What was going on? Were you about to meet Cher? Hardly.

Because dreams are symbols, you need to ask yourself where

you've seen this symbol before or what it might mean to you. Let's push another assumption forward. Maybe one of your favorite expressions when people irritate you is: "They are getting under my skin." See where the tattoo is taking you? Nothing can "get under your skin" more indelibly than a tattoo. To a person who doesn't like tattoos, the appearance of a symbolic design in the skin could be a strong call to pay attention to an emotional irritation.

Let's push a bit further and look at the face of Cher in this dream tattoo. Once more we're going to make an assumption to complete our example. What if you have a mother-in-law who is tall and slender, has a youthful appearance and long, black, dyed hair? Wouldn't there be a high possibility that this mother-in-law might have something to do with whatever is "getting under your skin"? If the foregoing suggestions were correct, the dream would probably be calling you to examine a troublesome irritation involving your mother-in-law that you're not paying attention to right now.

Now let's look at one of those dream experiences that truly terrify people. When we find monsters tromping through the bedroom at two in the morning, we can't help but be frightened. However, often the meaning of the experience is unexpected. For example, many horror film buffs are surprised to discover that Mary Shelley's original concept of the monster Frankenstein began as a dream of the author. While we've turned vampires and similar creatures into sci-fi movie material, some began as nightly reveries given for insight.

Have you noticed how horror movies both terrify and fascinate people? The attraction/fear arises from how these symbols operate in our dreams. Monster figures are generally symbols of our capacity to contemplate evil as well as our ability to do destructive deeds. They come in the night to make us aware of an aspect of our behavior we have ignored. While it's a horrible truth to admit, all of us carry the ability to do violent deeds. And though the dream beasts frighten us, they also attract us, because they release the fear or rage or some other emotion within us.

As was somewhat true of Mary Shelley's Frankenstein, we can't kill our own monsters as much as starve them to death. Attack won't stop them, as these creatures feed on violence. Rather, we must eradicate them through the redeeming love of Christ. While we do not often think of the blood of Christ in this context, Jesus' death on the cross has the power to displace these terrible symbols as redemption comes to our own lives. No conscientious person would ever compare the redeeming death of Jesus to the hideousness of the evil monsters in our dreams, yet there is a similarity in the picture of the beaten, broken condition of His bloody body hanging from the cross. As we look at Jesus suffering His pain for us, the image of His brokenness begins to dispel the terrible possibilities we discover in ourselves. For twenty centuries, sadists, alcoholics, child molesters, prostitutes, and countless people with lesser problems have been transformed as the image of Jesus dying on that cross pushed away their destructive tendencies.

THE PROCESS FOR DREAM EXPLORATION

As you come to understand the relationship between the shapes in a dream and your immediate daily life, you will often realize what the dream is telling you. Here are four steps to help you carry your exploration further:

1. Scrutinize the Symbols

Remember, signs and symbols aren't the same thing. A sign has only one meaning, while a symbol has profound layers of depth, conveying many levels of meaning. For example, a key ring is simply an organizer for keys to your house, office, car, and so on. If lost, there's no great pain. You simply get a new one. Is that true of a wedding ring? Not on your life! A wedding ring reminds you of the day of your wedding, subsequent anniversaries, children, and a million precious memories. Dreams are like a wedding ring.

Your task is to study, think, feel, meditate, and release the hidden meanings in a dream event. At first, it will seem impossible to wiggle your way inside the meaning, but don't get frustrated. Let the task be fun. Relax and play with the symbols until they open with unexpected direction.

In one of Robert Wise's dreams he encountered a woman in his congregation passing out lemons. Robert knew the woman well and didn't particularly like her because she had always been a difficult person. He quickly saw an important connection. The woman consistently left a "sour taste" in everyone's mouth. Lemons were a good symbol to describe how this person affected people.

However, the longer he thought about the dream, the more disturbed he became. Something else was working in this scenario and he had missed the meaning. Robert remembered that his dream was about him, not this woman. Abruptly he realized why she bothered him so much. They were much alike! The dream was telling him to pay attention to the way in which *he* left an acid taste in other people's mouths!

Scrutinizing a symbol is learning to allow the layers of meaning to surface.

2. Set the Symbol Free

Remember: the dream is not a puzzle to be solved as much as a mystery to be explored.

When our sleeping experiences terrify us, it's hard to get our thumping hearts to slow down. But we must remind ourselves that our task is to get beyond and behind the symbols that frightened us. Sometimes the answer will pop up later when we are driving down the street or walking across our backyard.

If you're having a struggle figuring out how these symbols work, let us give you a suggestion. Reading and thinking about poetry can help you get inside the symbolic world. The words, descriptions, and phrases attempt to take you to another place in your life's journey where meaning and values open in new and unexpected ways. Take a line from any poem, such as Robert Frost's description of two roads in a forest and what it means to take the one less traveled, and allow the symbols to roam around in your mind. The exercise will help you think symbolically.

After reading Frost's poem, a person might ask himself, "What are the less-traveled roads I've taken and what difference has this made in my life?" The person could ponder how these unexpected decisions change where he or she is today. In the same way, you can develop insight into your dream symbols as you allow them to lead you down a similar trail.

3. Don't Censor Yourself

You've probably seen some wild movies, but your inner dream mechanism can outdo them all! Dreams have no restraints and may often select the most bizarre, unexpected scenarios. Of course, scary expressions will frighten you. Also, the structure of the dream can shift in crazy, seemingly random ways, but that's because the meaning is conveyed most vividly in that extreme form. Don't feel threatened when your dreams take on strange forms and shapes.

We must allow our dreams to tell us whatever they wish.

Unfortunately, many of us have a tendency to give everything in our life a "face-lift" with a "Sunday-go-to-meeting" twist that leaves us in the best possible light—and that's why we struggle to make sense out of our dreams! They are honest while we prefer disguises. Instead, let the truth roll out!

4. Check the Lost-and-Found Department

Who hasn't lost something that is important to him only to find it in the most obvious place? Once we've located our lost contact lens or whatever, we wonder how we could have missed seeing the lens when the location is now so clear. The meanings of dream symbols are exactly the same.

Generally a dream confronts us with what we have hidden from ourselves. We keep the shadow side of our personality under wraps, and dreams push us to pay attention to what is already under our noses. Only as we work for a consistent and extended period of time will we begin to see the obvious truth we have avoided.

WHAT CAN I DO WITH
WHAT FRIGHTENED ME?

As strange as it might seem, you can learn to talk with these symbols and prompt them to release meaning and purpose. You need to develop the habit of writing down your dreams the moment you wake up. Dreams are like bubbles quickly gone. Robert Wise recommends keeping a notepad and a pencil next to the bed every night. Don't move until you've written down every detail of the last dream you remember before waking up.

Here's a method Robert Wise has often used with people attempting to encounter hidden messages in a dream symbol.

First, get out a sheet of paper and a good pen or pencil. You are going to write a dialogue as if you were writing a book. You will be writing both sides of the conversation so make sure you have plenty of paper. You don't want to break the spirit of the experience once it begins.

Second, before starting a conversation with some symbol in the dream, go back and reexperience the dream with as much vividness as you can muster. Feel it. Roll around with all of the symbols until you are back inside the events.

Third, pray that the Holy Spirit will help you. Jesus Christ is the Lord of your dreams. Allow Him to help you journey down difficult roads. The presence of God helps expose content as well as heal the wounds the dream may represent. Let Jesus assist you and be with you as you chat with the lightbulb or the frozen pond or other symbol in your dream.

Fourth, start talking to the dream symbol by writing questions on the paper in front of you. Don't worry that you're doing something strange or peculiar. You're not playing with evil or testing the limits of your faith. Jesus is with you, and dream symbols are part of you. The way you access their meaning is through this conversation, to a friend. Occasionally, someone will ask, "But what if something frightening or evil appears in my dream? Could I be talking with the devil?" Our response is that it is a reflection of something in your personality. The real question is, "How does that symbol reflect an experience or encounter in your *own* life that you should examine?" Don't worry. You're not talking to the devil; you are exploring an aspect of your life. We all do this when we have any kind of conversation with ourselves. It's a way of getting in touch with what we feel.

Consider the following. With your mind in a contemplative mode, you might write:

"Hello, Mr. Symbol. May I talk to you?"

Now let your imagination produce what it will. The symbol might answer, "Yes, I am here to speak to you."

"You appeared in my dream. I wondered why you were there."

"The answer lies in paying attention to the context. Go back and examine all the other facets of this dream. Look at what I am doing."

"Thank you," you might reply, "but can you tell me more directly why you are in my dream?"

"Yes. I have come to give you an insight you are missing."

See how a dialogue works? Even though you are carrying on both ends of the conversation, your spontaneous creativity will produce the results you need.

After you've written your initial inquiry, write whatever immediately comes to mind as a response. Try to stay in neutral and let the responses flow out of your unconscious. Keep writing questions and answers as long as is necessary. Eventually, you will get a grasp of the message.

Another form of inquiry is to reenter the dream. Imagine yourself going back inside the experience and talking with the various figures. You may want to set up conversations by inviting the dream figures to sit down and enjoy a cup of coffee with you (in your imagination, of course). Sound strange? Not at all. The adventure can be quite exciting.

If going back inside the dream seems too frightening, don't feel alone. Many people dread a reentry experience. Remember to invite Jesus Christ to go with you as your healing Friend and Defender. Giving your imagination complete freedom, allow Him to walk by your side.

This process will help you walk up to the monsters, people who have died, and other sources of fear and confront them. You will be ready to dialogue with the frightening subjects as you walk through the doors they are trying to open for you.

ADDITIONAL HELP

We have only scratched the surface. Dream interpretation is a vast subject that can take you into a fascinating world, resulting in wholeness and a deepened sense of purpose. Even though nightmares may look and feel like an army of Viking invaders crashing into your bedroom, in time the attackers may actually turn out to be admirers, bringing in armloads of help for your life.

One word of caution. Never allow someone who has a dream about you to manipulate you. In addition, avoid letting anyone give false direction to you based on his or her interpretation of your dream. More than a prediction of future events, dreams often confirm what we sense is not right or crack open a small door that may reveal new insight. We must remember that some dreams are not decipherable.

If you'd like to know more about exploring your dream world, we have listed books we've found helpful to people in Appendix B. You might want to check out their contents. For a special Christian approach to understanding dreams, consider studying *Windows of the Soul* by Paul Meier and Robert L. Wise (Thomas Nelson Publishers).

Now is the time to stop the fears chasing you at night. You can—and you will always be delighted you did!

Joel 2:28 says, "Your old men will dream dreams,/your young men will see visions"(NIV). Our dreams can lend much-needed insight into the meaning of our fears and what might be blocking us from becoming all God wants us to be. Consider exploring your dreams to quell your fears.

ELEVEN

Fear and Food

The Bible is a source of great inspiration in times of trouble, but it also has some startling Scriptures that are not so comforting. Consider Proverbs 23:2: "And put a knife to your throat,/ If you are a man of great appetite." Before you run to the cutlery drawer, consider the verse to be a warning that our appetites can be deadly. A woman named Marybelle Carlson shows how.

Several years ago Marybelle came in to talk with Stephen Arterburn. He couldn't avoid noticing that Marybelle had to be at least fifty pounds overweight. As their discussion began, she seemed uncomfortable and evasive in talking about her problem; Marybelle would rather have discussed the weather.

"You appear to be hesitant about telling me why you really are here," Stephen finally said. "Would you like to be more explicit?"

Marybelle bit her bottom lip. "You work with addicts. Correct?"

"Yes," Stephen said.

"Well," Marybelle wavered, "my problem isn't drugs. It's—it's—food."

"You're addicted to food?" Stephen asked.

"You'd never know it if you had lunch with me. I eat small portions and nothing that's fattening. In fact, you'd probably use me as a model example of how people ought to dine."

"Yes." Stephen motioned for Marybelle to keep talking.

"The problem is what I eat during the other fifteen hours of the day. I never stop munching. I cram my mouth full of potato chips and candy bars. I don't eat one cookie every now and then." Marybelle looked down at the floor. "I eat an entire bag of chocolate-chip cookies at one sitting. In the evening I can sit down and devour a quart of ice cream in minutes." She patted her stomach. "I'm a closet eater. That's why I've turned into such a blimp!"

"Anything make you afraid?" Almost impulsively Stephen asked what he had asked hundreds of others with eating problems.

"Oh, no!" the woman insisted. "If there's anything I'm not, it's apprehensive."

FEARFUL EATING

Was Marybelle's assertion correct? Absolutely not.

Stephen asked her to talk about her past to help both of them understand Marybelle's compulsive eating problem. Slowly, a painful story emerged. Marybelle lived through four years of an abusive relationship in a terrible marriage. Finally, the pain of her marriage proved to be too great. Then, a year after the divorce, Marybelle's mother discovered she was dying of cancer.

Marybelle's childhood family had been the center of her life.

Nothing was more fun than sitting at Sunday dinner around a table piled high with food. Through the years her mother remained the center of the family constellation with all the brothers and sisters circulating around her. Marybelle's world seemed perfect, but during the two years of her mother's illness, the center of the circle disintegrated. When her mother finally died in the hospital, Marybelle's life dropped into a black hole.

Marybelle described her constant eating as an attempt "to fill up a bottomless pit at the center of my life." The implication was clear. She was using food to fill a vast space left by the explosion of fear!

The demise of Marybelle's marriage and the death of her mother filled her with a fear of emptiness. She thought, *My life is like an empty gas tank, and I just can't stand it*. She started eating compulsively. In addition, the more she ate, the less people recognized Marybelle. Layers of fat covered the youthful, attractive woman who was turning herself into a completely different person. The shattered pieces of her existence remained so fragmented that Marybelle had lost the ability to recognize one of the most important facts of her life. From the start of every morning to the end of the day, Marybelle lived a terrified existence!

EATING OUR WAY OUT

While there are many reasons to overeat, fear remains a haunting motivation that can kill any diet or weight control program and create a powerful addiction. Compulsive eaters are often addicted to food in much the same way as alcoholics are to drinking. No matter what they profess, they can't stop consuming food compulsively until they address the issues of the heart.

In the Alcoholics Anonymous program, strugglers experience

genuine change when they turn their lives over to a "higher power," which for us (the authors) is the God of the Bible. People with eating disorders are no different. It's imperative that they have the help of their heavenly Father to thwart the work of fear in their lives. One aspect of this problem, which makes it so difficult to handle, is the subtlety of fear. Such people need the assurance of the hand of God resting on their shoulders, assisting them to pay attention to what is really going on when they sit down at the dinner table. Nothing's easier than reaching for a second . . . and a third . . . and a fourth helping during supper.

While Marybelle Carlson was a compulsive eater, many other apprehensive people are anorexic or struggle with bulimia. These three eating disorders touch millions of lives.

Anorexics starve themselves, often keeping their weight at least 20 percent below their ideal body weight. Strangely, like Marybelle, these underfed strugglers are actually hungry for love and in need of feeling control over something—even if it is their own demise. Paradoxically, anorexics are so starved for affection they give up attempting to satisfy hunger. They have the potential to literally starve themselves to death, and 15 percent of them do.

On the other hand, bulimics compulsively overeat and then purge themselves of this excessive amount of food. They may use laxatives, diet pills, or self-induced vomiting to clear their stomachs. The most destructive part of their problem is that purging starts an endless cycle. Once they are empty, bulimics are driven to eat again and then they purge once more. The endless cycle keeps rolling *over them*. They need help in getting in touch with the fact that they are trying to purge anxiety out of their systems. They may have a simple problem that they are scared to face, such as being enmeshed with Mother. Bulimics vomit their "situations," and eventually they can die from an electrolyte imbalance caused by the vomiting.

The problem? In all cases, it is fear!

FACING THE TRUTH

Marybelle's initial reticence to discuss her problem is typical of how overeaters fear facing their problem. They tend to see themselves as too heavy or thin (depending on the illness), but in either case, the strugglers deny the reality of their emotional situation. When Stephen asked Marybelle to be more specific, he was pushing her to stop denying the problem and recognize the truth. Ephesians 4:15 encourages us to speak "the truth in love" (NIV), which is what Stephen did when he told her she was overeating because she was afraid to face her real problem.

We must face the truth about how fear has worked under our skin, either distorting or diminishing our weight. Every form of therapy to correct addiction begins with facing the facts about our need.

Scripture tells us that God puts a high premium on the truth. Psalm 51:6 says our heavenly Father wants us to have "truth in the innermost being,/ And in the hidden part You will make me know wisdom." The Christian faith urges us to seek complete consistency with what God is saying. We may have to probe and push to get in touch with the truth, but honesty is the way to start climbing out of the pit.

THE ADDICTIVE CYCLE

The addictive cycle that Marybelle Carlson has bought into spins in this order:

- Denial
- Emotional pain
- Food that fuels the process
- The cost (weight gain and other costs)
- Self-loathing, followed by:
- More denial
- More pain
- More food (and the cycle goes on and on)

Do these steps sound frighteningly familiar? Do you have a sense that this cycle is true for you, but you'd just as well jump over the rest of this chapter rather than think about it *now*? We understand, but those tendencies give the cycle energy. You must pay attention to the problem *right now*. Here are five steps that will help you get off this Ferris wheel:

Step One: Stop Denying

While we may have a bundle of good excuses tucked away in our memories to justify every aspect of our problems, we can't get well until we stop kidding ourselves. Renewal begins when we allow the facts to be the facts. While Marybelle wouldn't have wanted to say the words out loud, she was struggling with a *love hunger*.

The problem began with Marybelle's divorce. She had anticipated a husband like her loving father. Because of her great respect and admiration for the elder Carlson, Marybelle never anticipated her husband deceiving and running around on her. When she discovered his adultery, the truth nearly destroyed Marybelle. The man had been critical, demanding, unemployed much of the time, and a real cad on top of it all! Obviously,

Marybelle's need for love and appreciation became enormous. While admitting a need for love can be extremely difficult, it is the first step out of our addiction.

Step Two: Face the Emotional Pain

Being honest about the depth of our emotional pain is extremely difficult. No one wants to get in touch with the root of the pain system, since this renews the loss and deprivation that we're trying desperately to avoid.

Generally our apprehension twists our opinion of ourselves, leaving us with low self-esteem. Even though our personal accomplishments may be of considerable scope, we tend to see ourselves in a diminished and insignificant position. The result is emotionally devastating.

We must learn that self-esteem is a gift only we can give ourselves. Rather than a product of accomplishment, enduring self-esteem rests on a sense of self-worth intrinsically ours because we are children of God. We have value because the heavenly Father has placed us in this world as His special envoys. We must recognize and accept this fact as true. Whether the president of the United States or a dishwasher, we are of supreme value in God's sight. Recognizing that fact is one of the most important steps we can take to break out of emotional pain. Experiencing unconditional love from good friends over a long period of time also reinforces our feelings of self-worth.

Step Three: Recognize That Food Fuels the Ferris Wheel

The addictive process is an endlessly turning wheel until something breaks the cycle. For the alcoholic, the chemical content of alcohol keeps the wheel moving. Food addicts have to accept the fact that food can have a similar effect on them.

Let's enumerate a number of the effects food can have. First, *food can kill pain.* Often people overeat because feeling full gives them a sense of well-being, which pushes away the gnawing anxiety they felt before the meal. Unfortunately, the effects of consistently overeating pile up around the waistline and the overeaters don't like the way they look. They are actually punishing themselves by becoming unattractive and endangering their health.

Second, *food also has a tranquilizing effect.* When we eat, blood sugar levels rise and neurochemicals called endorphins are released to give us a sense of well-being. After a few minutes of trotting, runners often experience a similar pleasant sensation. Food has actually turned into a tranquilizer. The quest for this feeling of well-being turns people into food addicts.

Third, *food can distance us from others.* People who were sexually abused or felt the intense pain of a broken love relationship find that eating excessively can put enough fat around them to keep members of the opposite sex away from them. Consequently, they protect themselves from any further abuse or unexpected rejection.

An oral addiction can also take on many other forms. Smoking, excessive talking, using profanity, grinding teeth—all can be expressions of the same pain. In each of these activities an addictive agent is fueling the Ferris wheel of our addiction.

If you are caught in this swirl of confusion, you must put food back in its proper place. You cannot allow the pleasantness of eating to distort what you actually require for your life.

Step Four: Face the Payoff

Fear forces people with eating disorders into an emotional bind. Sufferers may be forced into isolation and lose meaningful relationships with other people. They feel unworthy to be full participants in a normal life. The cost is high and humiliating.

People feel guilty about their purging and gorging behavior. They also feel guilty because they cannot control their eating. Even worse is the shame lurking underneath the fear. The shame that originated in their childhood is now a dark sense of worthlessness. And nothing is more difficult to bear than shame. This degrading emotion eats away all remaining self-respect and leaves the person feeling naked before the watching world. And as overweight people grow larger, they must carry the double shame of their extreme weight and its degrading appearance. Addiction specialists feel that nearly all addictions arise from experiences of shame or lack of connectedness—or both.

Step Five: Admit the Self-Loathing

As fear drives people from guilt to shame, it also affects the way they see themselves. In contrast to self-respect, overeaters develop self-hate. Although they may not be aware of the fact, they have started functioning in a highly self-destructive manner. Bulimic purging is one way to get rid of the fearful aspects of their lives. One of Dr. Meier's patients kept vomiting throughout her marriage; she was symbolically trying to rid herself of her emotional feelings about her controlling, abusive husband. Once she finally divorced her unfaithful, physically and sexually abusive husband, the vomiting stopped. Binges and purging are also ways that bulimics are destroying themselves. As bizarre as this repressed logic may be, millions of people do not face the self-hate that is causing their problems.

Of course, despising themselves enlarges the emotional emptiness they have been feeling for so long. Love hunger deepens, forcing the addictive cycle forward. These sufferers are helplessly entangled in a terrible process that can destroy their lives. Even though they make promises to adjust their eating behavior, nothing changes because they have failed to see the whole cycle for what it is—a process!

We noted earlier that Marybelle Carlson's reluctance to face her problem started her trouble. Denial keeps you in the addictive cycle. Stop letting your emotions talk you out of facing the truth—*right now.* Fear may have been wrecking your life, but you can start destroying the demolition process right now. In the space below, jot down the truth. What addictions do you struggle with? Food, alcohol, work, achievement, talking, exercise, smoking? You must stop denying the facts if you are going to break the addictive relationship.

The Payoff

After Marybelle's discussion with Stephen, a counselor helped the young woman face the addictive cycle, and she recognized the truth about the patterns controlling her life. By discovering how each part of the addictive cycle worked, she slowly dismantled her tendencies and got off the Ferris wheel. After several sessions she understood how guilt had turned into shame, causing her to camouflage herself behind layers of fat.

Finally, one afternoon Marybelle faced the most important truth of all. Bright sunlight shone through the windows of Stephen's office as Marybelle talked.

After several minutes she said, "My fear of facing the pain and suffering caused by the losses in my life was at the bottom of my addiction to food . . . The divorce was horrible, but when my mother died, I knew I was truly alone in this world. The worst fear of all was the sheer emptiness." With those words, Marybelle destroyed the addictive cycle in her life. She made a commitment to become part of a support group and also to reconnect with good friends.

Facing and accepting our worst fears and then moving into the future is one of the ways our heavenly Father sets us free from the past. When Marybelle was able to talk about fearing emptiness and did something about it, she was on her way to becoming a whole person.

Members of Alcoholics Anonymous and Overeaters Anonymous use the Serenity Prayer that Reinhold Neibuhr wrote: "God, grant me the serenity to accept the things I cannot change, courage to change the things I can, and the wisdom to know the difference."

Possibly these words will be helpful as you explore the hidden side of your inner world. Praying the Serenity Prayer can help break the destructive link between fear and food and put that destructive Ferris wheel to rest.

PART 3

Nothing to Fear . . .
but Fear Itself—
Building for the Future

TWELVE

Power from a Pill

Of all the creations of our miraculous God, the brain must be the most complex and extraordinary. Running on chemicals and electricity, the brain is a delicate organ in need of constant maintenance through our diet, exercise, water intake, and mental exercises. An amazing fact about the brain is that it has developed a way to repair itself. The brains of brilliant people have found substances and compounds that can assist the brain in this healing. These substances and compounds are a gift from God. The following is a case in point.

Gary Case seemed to have everything any thirty-four-year-old could want. He had a healthy history; although his father died when Gary was a child, his mother soon remarried a kind, gracious stepfather and Gary grew up as a happy child. School proved to be a pleasant season. In due time, he joined the church and became a Christian.

At twenty-two years of age, Gary married Anna, a wonderful, loving wife who gave him the supportive attention he needed.

With a good job and a gracious wife, Gary should have been set for life.

Unfortunately, Gary Case kept contemplating death, and fearing life itself.

Somewhere around age sixteen, Gary started to think about dying. He probably had a mild depression at that time but wasn't fully aware of the problem. The depression expanded with time, and his fear of dying increased. While his external life was going great, Gary's internal world kept sliding downhill. Without any apparent reason, Gary Case increasingly thought about dying until paradoxically his prayers became constant petitions for God to let him slip away.

Gary's problem had become serious when he came to see Dr. Paul Meier. His depression had started to affect his job, and Gary's wife hovered over him in constant fear he might take his life. After several minutes of talking, Dr. Meier asked Gary an important question that determined the direction his treatment would take.

"Have any of your family members ever struggled with depression?" Paul asked.

Gary nodded. "I'd say at least half of my relatives have had similar problems."

Gary's depression was probably caused by a genetic chemical imbalance.

KEEPING THE PROBLEM IN PERSPECTIVE

Most of this book has been about how you can solve your own issues or, with the help of a therapist, go beyond what you considered possible. However, there are times (as in Gary Case's situation) when drug therapy makes the difference. In this chapter, we are not suggesting what you ought to do specifically to obtain results. Those matters are between you and your personal physician. Our task is to help you put the use of drugs into a perspective that can help you know how to respond when medical assistance is needed, but let's be clear: *we are not offering specific guidance for any individual.*

The use of drugs to assist in mental problems is a relatively recent practice. For centuries, mental patients had been locked up in wards and forgotten. No one saw much hope for many forms of mental illness. Then, in the mid-1950s, medical progress broke down the barred doors with the discovery that Thorazine could produce amazing results for people with anxiety and psychosis. This drug helped to regulate the dopamine within the patient's brain.

At the same time, if drugs aren't prescribed correctly, they can backlash with devastating impact. In some patients, Thorazine had devastating side effects, like lowering blood pressure or causing neurological damage that produces weird movements of the arms and legs. It was clear the right conditions were extremely important. In this chapter, we want to explore those situations.

THE RIGHT DOCTOR UNDER THE RIGHT CIRCUMSTANCES

When most Americans are hit with anxiety problems, they turn to their local family physician rather than seeing a psychiatrist. While this would seem to be an appropriate response, it often leads to significant problems; the family physician may not be fully equipped to recognize both the negative and the positive effects of some drugs.

For example, many general physicians prescribe Xanax for

patients who complain about severe anxiety or panic attacks. Xanax is very appealing because of the immediate, total relief it brings in as short a time as ten minutes. This "magic pill" removes the symptoms of panic attacks for eight hours, so after that it is natural to take another pill. By swallowing a pill three times a day, sufferers immediately become free of the gnawing fear that had haunted them—or so it seems!

While Xanax can be quite helpful under the proper conditions, it is also a highly addicting benzodiazepine medication. Anyone taking the medicine three times a day for a significant period of time may become addicted to Xanax and will soon need four, then five or more a day. Because the drug numbs feelings, users also become less insightful. They may be living an anxiety-free life, but they are less in touch with their feelings. The doctor may have meant well, but the results in these cases aren't positive.

Serotonin antidepressants are the safest and best medications for anxiety and panic. They can be taken throughout life if needed and are still not addictive, but they take ten weeks to reach a peak. Consequently, panic will continue until they kick in.

Dr. Meier always wants his patients to be on the safest and best medications, but he knows he would feel horrible if even one of his patients had to endure another hour of panic and pain. Therefore, he has his own approach. Let's go back to Gary Case's situation, right after he admitted having relatives who struggled with similar issues.

Dr. Meier immediately knew a strong possibility existed that Gary Case's problem wouldn't be cured by counseling alone. When a hereditary problem exists, it usually means that some chemical imbalance has created a predisposition toward depression or anxiety or both.

Meier leaned over and put his hand on Gary's shoulder. Looking him squarely in the eye, Paul said, "You've had the last anxiety attack you will ever have to experience."

"W—what?" Gary stammered. His eyes widened. "You're kidding me."

"No," Paul said. "I'm quite serious. You are going to be well."

Gary shook his head. "You must know I've already been to a number of counselors about this problem. And I've taken every herbal remedy in the book to make me stop being fearful, but nothing has helped."

Paul shook his head. "I understand because I work with these cases often. Counseling is important, but it's not what you need."

"I have had people at the church pray for me," Gary insisted. "I've read the Bible."

"The Bible and prayer are extremely important," Paul agreed. "I've been studying the Bible every day of my life since I was ten years old. Having people pray for you helps, but something more is needed in your case. You need to take the right medication, one that will not numb your feelings or make you addicted."

The Bible says, "In a multitude of counselors there is safety" (Prov. 24:6 NKJV). Dr. Meier relied on a combination of four medications to get Gary through this problem. Effexor-XR is helpful in reducing anxiety as well as building serotonin (which reduces depression and anxiety) and norepinephrine (which reduces depression and increases energy, memory, concentration, and sexual enjoyment). His second prescription was Neurontin, which builds up GABA (the natural gamma amino butyric acid produced by the brain) and relieves anxiety. Dr. Meier also prescribed Wellbutrin-SR, which builds up norepinephrine. Finally, he gave Gary some Clonazepam that he could take as needed until the other medications kicked in.

Effexor-XR probably would have been enough by itself, but Gary was highly suicidal, and Dr. Meier wanted to play it safe. He realized he could always drop the Clonazepam within a month and one or two of the other medications when Gary had been feeling better for approximately six months.

Within three weeks Gary's preoccupation with death vanished and his depression floated away. He was back where God meant him to be. Within ten weeks, Gary told Dr. Meier he had never been so happy or excited about life.

The right drugs probably saved his life.

THE PRECISE MEDICINES

To help determine if drugs might be useful in your situation, we will review some of the most significant medications to treat fears, phobias, and anxieties. By comparing and contrasting different medications, you will be able to develop your own viewpoint on how medicines can help.

Clonazepam

The least addicting form of benzodiazepine, Clonazepam is often recommended when clients feel a panic attack is coming or when they have developed severe anxiety. Like Xanax, Clonazepam will relieve the panic attack within ten or fifteen minutes and keep it away for eight hours, but Clonazepam is significantly less addicting. Thus, this drug has an almost immediate effect on fear problems.

Sufferers with a phobia of flying often need medication to stop their emotions from exploding when they enter an airplane. A dose of Clonazepam taken an hour before boarding the plane will help passengers get beyond their phobia. As we saw in chapter 9, some pastors experience a similar problem—they have panic attacks before they preach. Some people, like Norman, are able to overcome this problem with desensitization. Others need the medication. Again, a pill taken an hour before speaking settles their nerves, and they are able to preach without anxiety.

Effexor-XR

One of the most important chemicals in your body for maintaining stability and well-being is serotonin. In the 1960s, when Dr. Meier was an "alumni distinguished graduate fellow" at Michigan State University, he wrote his master's thesis on this recently discovered chemical substance that allows thinking to occur. Serotonin operates in the synapses (the microscopic spaces between cells), facilitating the passage of electrical impulses. In addition, this natural chemical in our body is a necessity if we are going to feel happy, sleep well, and live relatively fear-free. Your car can't run without gasoline, and your brain can't run without serotonin.

Serotonin isn't something that can be consumed. Rather, the brain manufactures the substance out of the tryptophan in our diets. Bananas, turkey, other meats, and dairy products are good sources of tryptophan. Most antidepressants help our brains hold on to this natural serotonin, since we must have this substance if we are going to function properly.

Effexor-XR fits this need and is particularly helpful to patients struggling with severe anxiety. Zoloft and Celexa are quite similar, as they help the brain retain the serotonin it is producing. These two drugs do not cause weight change but Effexor-XR can result in some weight loss. Two other well-known antidepressants, Paxil and Remeron, often cause as much as thirty pounds of weight gain. (Paxil CR was released in 2002. It promises to eliminate many of the side effects, including weight gain.) On the other hand, these two drugs can be quite helpful in working with anorexic cases where weight gain is important. Prozac also works very well and is usually "weight neutral," but because some patients complain that it seems to numb their emotions, Dr. Meier usually tries Effexor-XR, Zoloft, or Celexa first.

These drugs are all serotonin-building medicines and each can eliminate panic attacks and severe anxiety about 75 percent of the time—but they each take about ten weeks to have full effect. If you fall into the other 25 percent, one of the other serotonin antidepressants will probably work. If Effexor-XR doesn't work for a patient, Dr. Meier will prescribe Zoloft; if that drug doesn't work, he prescribes Celexa, and if the patient still does not receive relief, he will turn to Prozac. Again, each one has about a 75 percent chance of helping.

Effexor-XR, Zoloft, Celexa, and Prozac are not addictive, and therefore, can be taken for a lifetime. Some people only need them for a year, but those with a family history of depression and anxiety may need them lifelong. A person only needs to take a serotonin medication once a day, like a vitamin. It doesn't create a false high, but just facilitates our process of healing ourselves.

Why doesn't our brain produce enough serotonin on its own? Serotonin receptor sites, or "suckers," pull the serotonin out of the cell synapses and keep the balance in the brain under control. When these suckers work too well and take too much serotonin, the proper level is reduced to a low point and we start to feel anxious and irritable. We don't sleep well and may drop into depression.

Some people's nervous systems work effectively until they experience anger, guilt, or stress or drink too much alcohol or smoke marijuana. Under those difficult conditions, the suckers overwork and imbalance follows. They need medical assistance.

Drugs like Zoloft or Celexa block the work of the suckers in the brain long enough to allow natural serotonin to accumulate at a normal level. They are called SSRIs, which stands for *selective serotonin reuptake inhibitors.*

The main difficulty with SSRI medicines is the time they take to do their work. A good psychiatrist will gradually build up the dosage to about 300 milligrams of Effexor-XR every morning, or about 100 to 200 milligrams of Zoloft daily, or about 40 milligrams of Celexa or Prozac. No one should take two SSRIs at the same time, hoping for a speedier effect. That could be dangerous.

After about a week or two, the patient will feel more normal and progress will increase up to a peak in the tenth week. As long as he is taking the medication, the client will feel normal, although a few people may find the medicine seems to quit working after several weeks. An increase in dosage generally puts them back on track, or they may need a different medicine.

GABA Medicines

GABA medications can function either immediately or within a few days. Most of the GABA (gamma amino butyric acid) medicines build up the normal supply of GABA in your brain. God gave us this chemical in our brains to help us feel calm and relaxed. While GABA medicines are mainly used as antiseizure drugs, they help relieve anxiety within a few hours to a few days. Neurontin, Topamax, and Depakote-ER are non-addictive and very rarely have any serious side effects; they are very helpful for anxiety, bipolar disorder, and social phobias. But they don't help depression significantly.

Topamax is beneficial with overweight patients because it decreases appetite as well as speeding up the patient's metabolism as he or she relaxes. Usually recipients lose a pound a week for twenty weeks and then stabilize at a twenty-pound weight loss. However, some of Dr. Meier's patients have lost as much as fifty or sixty pounds on Topamax. If you are prone toward kidney stones or glaucoma, you may want to avoid this drug.

With all GABA medicines, Dr. Meier usually starts with a low dosage and works his way toward what is best for the person. After a period of testing, patients generally end up on 3,000 milligrams a day of Neurontin, 200 milligrams a day of Topamax, or 1,000 to 1,500 milligrams a day of Depakote-ER.

Seroquel, Zyprexa, Risperdal, and Geodon

These are "major tranquilizers." Doctors generally don't use them for anxiety disorders unless the patient has severe insomnia, or when an antidepressant/Clonazepam combination is not enough or the patient is psychotic. Because one out of every thirty-three Americans lose touch with reality at some time in their lives, the problem is more common than most people recognize.

While these tranquilizers can produce amazing results, they also have some disadvantages. They take at least an hour to kick in, and, at first, often leave the client feeling extremely tired for an entire day. It is possible for these drugs to cause the patient to gain five to ten pounds and in some rare cases, forty or fifty pounds. Clonazepam, on the other hand, takes only about ten minutes to work, and it doesn't cause drowsiness. It may cause slight weight gain.

Seroquel, Zyprexa, Risperdal, and Geodon work by regulating the amount of dopamine in the brain, which helps us to relax, feel pleasure, and see reality more clearly. While too little of the substance can create problems like Parkinson's disease, too much dopamine causes insanity. Regulation is important.

Dr. Meier likes Seroquel the best because it works very well, it has the fewest side effects, and it usually causes only a few pounds of weight gain. Some obese patients actually lose weight on it. Zyprexa works very well but causes significant weight gain in many patients and may tip patients into adult onset diabetes, which usually clears up when they quit taking the drug. Dr. Meier often adds Topamax (which causes weight loss) to Zyprexa when Zyprexa is the best drug for someone, but weight gain is a concern.

Wellbutrin-SR

As important as serotonin is in creating normal function, norepinephrine does vital work as well; it communicates a sense of joy, motivation, energy, focus, memory, and pleasure in sex. Norepinephrine depletion results in depression. Wellbutrin-SR is helpful in treating this.

Although not used with epileptics, Wellbutrin-SR is a safe and powerful antidepressant but its effect on anxiety is limited.

Effexor-XR is the best antidepressant available today because it builds both serotonin *and* norepinephrine at the same time, and it helps defeat anxiety and depression, defuses phobias, and gives clients more energy. Wellbutin-SR can be given alone or along with any serotonin antidepressant.

St. John's Wort

A new miracle drug? A recently recognized cure for your fears? Hardly.

Sooner or later someone is going to recommend this herbal remedy as the cure for depression or anxiety. Should you buy it? Here are the facts. See what you think.

St. John's Wort does build up serotonin but only slightly. Actually, you pay more for the herb than you do for SSRI drugs.

And St. John's Wort has many negative side effects. It has been documented that two heart transplant patients who took it without notifying their doctors died from this medication. St. John's Wort cannot be mixed with any prescription serotonin medicines (like Prozac, Zoloft, Paxil, and so on), because it could cause death from "serotonin syndrome"—or too much serotonin in the system—which can affect the ability to walk and use limbs. In addition, only 20 percent of St. John's Wort products in health-food stores actually have the right amount of the right ingredients. Some have absolutely no St. John's Wort in them at all. Unfortunately, there is no regulation of these over-the-counter medicines.

The truth is SSRIs won't kill anyone, and 90 percent of the time they have no side effects.

People seem to think taking St. John's Wort produces some special "spiritual" effect because it is natural. The next time someone suggests the value of natural medications, you might remind them that arsenic and cyanide are also natural—but they won't get you further than the nearest graveyard.

A FINAL THOUGHT

We have considered many ways to defeat fear and will look at others. You can do more to stop your anxieties than you ever thought. However, when medication is needed—*it's needed!* If our bodies aren't producing the right chemicals in proper balance, we need to add medicines to restore order. Taking medical preparations is *not* a defeat of your faith or willpower. Remember: when the right drug is prescribed in the proper manner, consumption can be extremely valuable to your health. Medication is one of several God-given methods for coping with fear. If a medicine corrects a genetic chemical imbalance and helps you become a happier, more relaxed, more effective servant of God, *not* taking it would be a sin and a real shame. Pride makes us either want to do everything in our own strength or do nothing at all. Humility enables us to ask for the help of God, friends, Christian counselors, and sometimes even correctional medications. Dr. Meier plans to use Wellbutrin-SR the rest of his life to correct his genetic ADHD (Attention Deficit Hyperactivity Disorder).

Thirteen

The Divine Point
of View

Anyone can easily sit in a church sanctuary and make pious affirmations, but it is another thing to remember those convictions when the clock strikes midnight, the wind shakes the shingles on the roof, and the sound of footsteps seems to be coming from the back porch. Fear has a terrible way of scattering our beliefs and reducing our faith to words in the wind.

On September 11, 2001, the American way of life changed forever. Never before had an enemy attacked the continental shores of the United States. In the most populous city in America, foreign intervention struck two of the most significant buildings in the world. No longer were we an innocent people saved from the marching armies sweeping across Europe or the hordes of Genghis Khan arising from out of the east. We knew it was possible for any American to die from an enemy's attack. Fear had new meaning. It was personal, intimate, and immediate.

Facing and defeating fear is always an act of courageous faith. While our adrenaline-filled emotions scramble and our hearts beat as if they will explode, we need courage to stand against adversity and to maintain faith when everything we value appears ready to collapse. An enduring faith is a necessity if we are going to defeat fear.

Recently, the people in the sedate, historic city of Charlotte, North Carolina, learned a couple of jarring facts. Charlotte has two major atomic-energy power plants within twenty miles of each other that are beginning to use plutonium as an energy generator. Plutonium is also a highly explosive and radioactive fuel. In addition, the town of Charlotte has become the second largest financial district in the country with some of the largest banks in America.

Would kindly old Charlotte, with all of its southern charm, become a likely place for a strike if terrorists decided to attack this country again? Absolutely. Charlotte, the city of old Civil War stories, could be in the center of the conflict—as could many other cities in the United States that have nuclear power facilities. In places we would never have thought vulnerable, a new urgency has sprung up. Does believing in God help quell our fears?

STILLING THE STORM

More than a decade ago, Dr. Robert Wise went through a time of savage change when fear rocked everything in his life. During this difficult period, he took a forty-day retreat to do the Spiritual Exercises of St. Ignatius, which require a thirty-day period of total silence. Each morning he got up, took his Bible, went out into the woods, and spent the next eight hours in prayer, walking through the events in Jesus' life. Much to his surprise, these times of solitude were anything but subdued.

Robert quickly found himself plunged into spiritual conflict, which elevated the fears he brought with him to the retreat center.

HE WAS BEING TESTED TO THE LIMIT.

In the middle of the retreat, Robert studied the story of Jesus walking out on the Sea of Galilee to meet His apostles when their boat appeared ready to sink. Robert's spiritual exercises included using his imagination to place himself in the first-century events. He figuratively became a part of what occurred two thousand years ago, living in the biblical account as if he were one of the disciples' closest friends. He felt the storm rocking the boat and the disciples' fear that the craft would disintegrate and sink. Envisioning the apostle Peter's fearful face, Robert could sense the same apprehension he had known at age eighteen when he nearly drowned. Desperately clutching his Bible, Robert read in a new and personal way the reply Jesus made to Peter's terror: "Take courage, it is I; do not be afraid" (Matt. 14:27).

At that moment he realized the key issue in facing fear was not an abstract idea of simply believing. Far from a nebulous commitment to positive thinking, faith is the concrete commitment of saying *no to fear* and *yes to Jesus Christ*. Believers cannot simply say no to apprehension; they must say yes to the Master of the storm.

In the first chapter, we recognized that God's gift is hope! He did not intend for us to be timid people, but to live with an abiding sense of power, love, and self-control (2 Tim. 1:7). Those gifts weren't abstractions but came through the believers' personal encounters with Jesus Christ. To successfully defeat fear, we must live out that relationship.

How Shall We Say Yes?

As we mentioned in chapter 4, far from discounting fear, the Bible tells us the beginning of knowledge is the fear of God (Prov. 1:7). Intelligence begins when we recognize and accept the supreme place our heavenly Father has over all creation. We are to revere and worship Him above all else. Fear can become power when it helps us recognize how life is meant to be ordered and respected. Recognizing and respecting God's awesome power is what the Scripture means by the "fear of God." Faith begins with this yes!

As the 2002 Winter Olympics began in Salt Lake City, thousands who attended experienced a new dimension of how life has changed in America. More American military personnel were at the Olympic Games at that moment than were fighting in Afghanistan. The security arrangements and checkpoints proved to be nearly overwhelming. People complained about the enormous amount of time required to pass the metal detectors. Yet they filed into the games under completely safe circumstances because the American check system gave them confidence in the security. Faith had displaced fear. In the same way, recognizing our need for the protective hand of God is an act of faith.

Stephen Arterburn, the founder of Women of Faith Conferences, has held these events all over America. In November 2001, Stephen had a conference scheduled for Philadelphia. The September 11 attacks forced much rescheduling but the Philadelphia event went ahead on schedule. One of the speakers was Lisa Beamer.

By November, Americans knew the story of Todd Beamer. He had been a passenger in the fateful crash of one of the airplanes the terrorists commandeered. Rather than acquiesce and allow the airplane to be targeted into some nationally important sight like the White House, Todd Beamer and his fellow passengers attacked the terrorists. Talking on his cell phone to a supervisor of the phone company moments before the attack and airplane crash, he concluded by saying the now-famous words, "Let's roll." His brave response was another way to say yes.

As Lisa Beamer reflected on her dead husband's bravery, she noted that he had a choice to live in fear or hope. As a Christian man, Todd chose hope. Was it frightening to counterattack the terrorists bent on destroying the airplane and some unknown target? Of course! But saying yes to the hope God offers allows us to find transcendent faith, which helps put fears back into perspective.

FACING THE DARK

As a child, Robert Wise lived upstairs in his parents' home. His long, narrow bedroom had large attic spaces on each side of the walls. During the winter nights when the fierce winds blew and the temperature dropped, the house would crack and squeak, sounding as if some kind of sci-fi monster was waiting in the attic to leap out of the dark at any moment. Although he was not particularly religious and had no idea who God was, Robert would often pull the covers over his head and endlessly repeat the Lord's Prayer, hoping the intercessions would keep the monster from crashing through the wall. As an adult, he came to see that his childhood fears were a microcosm of how we live our entire lives. Once people become afraid, they turn to God, calling on Him for assistance. The truth is his childish prayers weren't so naive after all.

Is your life filled with situations that make you afraid? Of course, we are concerned about everything from falling down stairs to taking trips out of town. Snow and ice give us the shivers as much as getting a heatstroke in the summertime makes us sweat. Our lives contain a million and one reasons to call on God's help.

Often these fears don't go away because we base them on the solid possibility that we could get hurt or injured. Yet we must go on through these everyday situations. How do we live confidently? As Robert Wise did as a child, our praying and seeking God's help is an important part of making it from sunup to sundown. We need to put God into the situations we fear. Here's an exercise that can help:

Sit down and think about your fear. Imagine as completely as you can what it would be like to have your fear-filled event happen. For example, say you fear the possibility of falling on an icy sidewalk. Envision your feet slipping out from under you and feel yourself crashing against the ice. Of course, the fall automatically creates pain and disruption. A crash could break your hip. Let yourself feel the pain.

Now, go back and let's start over again. The divine point of view tells us God has His eye on everything happening in our lives. Jesus Christ always stands beside us. We don't need to slide off into fanciful thinking or magical interpretations to know that if God is watching us, He will make a divine difference. What changes might the presence of the Lord make in that fear-filled fantasy you just had? How would His all-encompassing love affect any accident you might have? Put that possibility in your imagination and envision the fall again. Feel the pain. Jesus Christ will lead you through this experience by sustaining you emotionally, guiding you with His love, and helping you find emergency aid. Feel His arms around you and His love as you go through this painful situation. Try this and see what a difference it makes. You have the ability to view situations you fear in a different light.

Are we only playing a game, spinning a fantasy? No, we are talking about a reality, the person of Jesus Christ. Worry and fear bother us so much because we allow them to use our imaginations against us. Faith offers a handle to turn the situation around. We can find a new way to envision the best rather than the worst.

The divine point of view creates new perspectives that thwart fear.

FEAR OF BEING OVERWHELMED

Many people are afraid because the life tasks before them seem overwhelming. Their hidden question is whether faithfulness will result in God giving them an oar larger than they can pull. Can they do what God asks of them?

They need to remember the conversation King David had with his son Solomon when he told Solomon to build the temple in Jerusalem. He said, "Be strong and courageous, and act; do not fear nor be dismayed, for the LORD God, my God, is with you. He will not fail you nor forsake you until all the work for the service of the house of the LORD is finished" (1 Chron. 28:20). If God asks something of you, He will be there to bring it to fulfillment. You can count on the Lord!

Dr. Paul Meier found this fact to be absolutely true. His father was a carpenter, and Paul expected to grow up and follow in his steps. But when he was sixteen years old, a surgical resident at his church invited Paul to come over for a conversation. Dr. Bob

Schindler had seen something special in Paul and wanted to encourage him to consider becoming a physician. In time, Dr. Schindler would become widely known as a missionary doctor. He encouraged Paul to memorize Proverbs 3:5–6: "Trust in the LORD with all your heart, / And do not lean on your own understanding. / In all your ways acknowledge Him, / And He will make your paths straight."

That night Paul awoke twice with surprising dreams. In the first, he heard Jesus Christ saying to him, "I want you to become a doctor." The dream was so intense Paul immediately decided to become what he felt God had called him to be. He would pursue medicine. In the second dream, Paul saw himself as an older person going from country to country, teaching people, and helping them become what God had ordained. His assumption was that God had called him to be a missionary doctor.

From that moment on, Paul approached his education with new seriousness, reading more broadly and studying harder, because the new mandate on his life left him feeling fearful. He worried whether he could face the challenge God had given him. The future had a frightening twist. As time went by, Paul felt a strong call to enter the field of psychiatry, which precluded going from country to country. Paul guessed his interpretation of the second dream must have been wrong.

Early in the 1990s, Paul Meier went with Robert Wise to Israel to work on the novels they were writing in the best-selling Millennium series. Robert had been traveling in Israel since the late sixties and often led tours. He and Paul traversed the entire country. Near the end of the tour, Paul attended a service with a messianic congregation in Jerusalem, whose membership was composed of Jews who had accepted Jesus as their Messiah.

Using earphones to hear a translation in English, Paul was worshiping in the synagogue at the moment the rabbi explained the congregation's current needs. "We have many believers in Yeshua [Hebrew for Jesus]," the rabbi explained, "but we need counselors. Today let us pray that God will send us a psychiatrist, a counselor, someone who can teach us about helping people with psychological problems."

The group began to pray, but Paul almost couldn't believe what he had heard. Following the service, he walked forward and spoke to the rabbi. "I am a psychiatrist," Paul said. "When do you want me to come?"

The rabbi was startled, obviously shocked.

The following year, Dr. Meier returned and trained lay counselors from all over Israel, helping the national messianic community expand their ministry. Those training sessions proved to be exciting and significant.

On the way back to the United States, Paul flew from Tel Aviv to Paris surrounded by people who didn't speak English. He felt disappointed—he always requested a seat in the middle to be able to talk with his fellow passengers—but the passengers beside him did not speak English.

Waiting to board the airplane for the eleven-hour trip from Paris to Chicago, Paul prayed, "Lord, please give me someone I can talk to or I'll go crazy from boredom." A few minutes later, a lovely blonde French lady with blue eyes, who spoke English fairly well, sat beside Paul. A conversation quickly followed as both persons shared facts about their lives. Paul remembers praying a silent word of thanks that went something like this: *Lord, I'm a happily married man, but she'll do just fine for someone to talk to during this trip. Help me to focus on her soul and not on her physical beauty.*

"Why are you going to Little Rock, Arkansas?" Paul asked. "Not much of a trip after being in Paris."

"Ten years ago I became a Christian," the young woman explained, "because a missionary from Little Rock gave me a book called *Happiness Is a Choice*. Have you ever read it?"

Paul chuckled. He had written the best-seller years before. "Oh?" he said. "I've heard of that book."

"As a result of this book, I am now a missionary in Lyon, France," the woman continued. "We have missionaries in France, but we need counselors. I hope my friend can help me find Dr. Paul Meier, as he needs to come and teach us."

Paul grinned. "I'm Paul Meier."

The woman refused to believe Paul until she looked at his passport. As a result of this amazing conversation, they set a time for Paul to return to France. Shortly after that training experience, he taught in Sweden, Norway, Denmark, Greece, Germany, Turkey, Peru, Russia, Cuba, and in Israel five more times. His second dream had been fulfilled! But even more important, Paul's apprehension about the calling God had given him proved empty. The God who called Paul was the God who handled the details. Obviously, an assignment to teach in a number of countries would frighten anyone, but the mission had unfolded in such a natural way, the teaching assignments felt easy and normal. Rather than being avalanched by the huge assignment, God had taken Paul a step at a time to success, which erased his fear.

If God asks you to perform a task, He will help you complete it! And these experiences will become some of the most exciting events of your life. You don't need to be afraid of being over-whelmed by God's call on your life. Amazing miracles happened to Dr. Meier on these trips that could fill additional chapters.

CHANGE YOUR GOAL

Apart from personal apprehension, probably one of the major fears in American society is failing on the job. A primary goal in American life is to make money, which means doing well at work. But how can such a goal not lead to a fear of failing? As a nation, we recognize the supreme importance of bringing home the paycheck every month. Today both men and women struggle with fears of faltering in their careers.

Obviously, our desire to succeed at any cost soon creates a collision of values with our faith. When such a clash occurs, a high percentage of the population choose their jobs over their Christian convictions. Those decisions create more of the fears people struggle with day after day.

What's the divine point of view on this problem? Change our goal! The Scripture is clear. The most important objective of our lives should be to become like Jesus Christ. The apostle Paul said, "One thing I do: forgetting what lies behind and reaching forward to what lies ahead, I press on toward the goal for the prize of the upward call of God in Christ Jesus" (Phil. 3:13–14). If Wall Street, the United Nations, Congress, and the marketplace in your community exchanged the goal of prospering for obtaining the high call of God in Christ, our world would become radically different and better—with less fear!

"But," you might quickly respond, "would such a decision mean God is going to protect us from all calamities and keep us from ever getting caught in a disaster like the towers' collapse on September 11?" Would Todd Beamer have completed his mission that day and still be alive? Our answer is emphatically *no*.

It's naive for Christians to presume upon God to protect them from the experiences and abuses that happen every day.

Good, faithful Christians inevitably get sick, have accidents, are abused, get killed on the highway, and are even destroyed in terrorist attacks. We have to make adjustments and learn to live with these fears. They are part of the normal fabric of human existence. But what would it look like to live beyond these problems? The apostle Paul described the possibility as clearly as anyone ever has: "Not that I speak from want, for I have learned to be content in whatever circumstances I am. I know how to get along with humble means, and I also know how to live in prosperity; in any and every circumstance I have learned the secret of being filled and going hungry, both of having abundance and suffering need. I can do all things through Him who strengthens me" (Phil. 4:11–13).

Economics shouldn't run our lives; Jesus Christ should.

NO LONGER ALONE

Fear of God provides a different context for our decisions, dreams, and goals. During his college years, Robert Wise became agnostic. Armed with the ideas of existentialism, he couldn't find God in this world. He graduated from college and went into the field of social work without any sense of divine direction. His no to faith in God put him in a completely different context. He didn't believe a God was checking on his behavior, his hopes, his intentions. He put both feet in a universe without God.

Did being an agnostic solve Robert's fear problems? Most certainly not. He felt alone in a hostile world. No help or assurance came from anywhere but himself. Loneliness became the order of the day. Nothing was left to abate fear.

Only as Robert accepted Christ, and came to see and believe the truth about God being a part of everything happening in the world, did he understand why the Scripture said faith was the start of intelligence. Knowing that every thought, action, and deed happened under the watchful eye of a God who understood his thoughts, wants, wishes, and actions changed Robert's perspective.

Psalm 111:10 says, "The fear of the LORD is the beginning of wisdom; / A good understanding have all those who do His commandments; / His praise endures forever." The passage suggests that one of the ways we express our fear of the Lord is by being obedient to what He asks. Faithfulness expresses the place of honor He holds in our lives. An obedient yes to Him is also one of the ways we defeat fear.

COURAGE AFTER THE STORM

This chapter began by recognizing that fear can disrupt faith but ends by affirming that faith can conquer fear. We not only have the capacity to live through stormy times, but God intends for us to go on living courageous lives after the tempest has blown through town.

We need to recognize that the evening television news report, the newspapers, and the gossip over the backyard fence aren't the final word on anything. Jesus taught us that in the beginning was the Word and the Word became flesh . . . and He was the Word! That's the communication we need to depend on. That's the divine point of view.

FOURTEEN

The View
from the Grave

How tall are you?" Joe Harris defensively asked Robert Wise. The elderly man appeared to be in his late seventies and was dressed in work clothes. Joe kept his lip stuck out as if he were looking for an argument.

For a moment Robert reflected on the strange question. "Around five-foot-seven," he finally replied. "Why?"

"Ever stand deep down inside a grave?" Joe asked. "You wouldn't even be able to see out. You're standing there six feet deep, ya know."

"Yes," Robert answered slowly. "So?"

"Reverend, I used to dig graves. Took my shovel and threw dirt out the top until I got down there on the bottom. I ain't even five-foot-six. I know what it's like to have a view from the bottom of the grave. I'm here to tell ya it sure don't give ya any comfort."

Joe Harris tried to sound indifferent and distant, but behind his words lurked a universal fear. One hundred percent of the human race eventually dies. At some time or another we all have to consider whether anything is ahead when our hearts stop beating. Often we lean back, put our feet up on the coffee table, and treat the question as if it is an issue for someone else, but we cannot avoid the personal and fearful nature of the question. Is there anything more?

Is That All There Is?

Somewhere between ages thirty-five and forty-five, we find that our personal issues shift. Before that point, the idea of dying is an abstraction with little individual meaning. We always see ourselves walking through the fire, missing the bullets, crawling out of wrecked cars, and bailing out of crashing airplanes. Other people die. Unless a personal situation forces us up against a near-death experience, we simply don't perceive dying as a personal reality. During midlife our perspective changes. Deep inside, we know imperishability is not a reality.

As midlife causes our psyches to veer, the issue is no longer *What am I going to do with my time?* but *Why am I doing "this" day after day?* We wonder if the way we work each day is truly worthwhile. The issue is meaning. At that point we realize we have only a limited amount of time left in this world. Once we recognize our tenure on earth will end, we confront the universal fear of dying.

Several years ago a popular song examined all the experiences of life and concluded after each verse, "Is that all there is?" The indifferent, hardened attitude of the singer made death sound inconsequential. When the movie actor Errol Flynn was dying, he is reported to have said callously, "Dying ain't so tough," closed his eyes, and was gone. Are these attitudes typical?

Far from it. *No one escapes facing the fear of death.*

If we are going to build for the future with confidence and

determination, we must have answers for what lies on the other side of the end of our days.

CONFIDENCE WHEN
THE GROUND IS FROZEN

Back in the eighties, Dr. Robert Wise traveled to the Soviet Union during the time Mikhail Sergeyevich Gorbachev was prime minister of the U.S.S.R. The winter had been hard and icy winds still swept down the frozen streets, but even in this world of atheistic Communism, Robert found many common people braving the weather to enter the Orthodox churches. People particularly seemed to anticipate the approaching religious holiday. Easter was coming.

After a few inquiries, Robert discovered why Easter was so important. Death has a central place in Soviet society. Joseph Stalin had ordered at least twenty million people killed as the Leninist revolution went on and on and on. Virtually no family escaped losing someone in those terrifying days of random killings and executions. Then during World War II, the Russian government purposely quit counting after they identified twenty million deaths that had been caused by the war with Germany. Stalin feared the people might turn on him if the recorded total of casualties increased, and another revolution would crush his government. The vast scope of death touched every town, village, street, and home in the Soviet Empire.

But now, even to this wintry tundra, Easter was coming. The Russians had a unique way of celebrating. On the night immediately before this most important day on the Christian calendar, Russians filed into their churches and the choirs sang mournful dirges. An atmosphere of despair hung over the congregation, but as midnight approached, the congregation filed out of the church. Each person held a candle, trudging through the front door of the church, singing the sad hymns. Then the church door slammed behind them with a mournful thud.

During the darkest hour of the night, this congregation in Moscow began a long journey around the church building. When they came back to the front, someone knocked on the door of the church but there was no answer. The congregants started around a second time and then again knocked with no response. The third time, the door still remained bolted shut. On the fourth return, as someone at the head of the procession started to knock the door flew open. A Russian priest leaped out and shouted with all his might, "Christ is risen!"

The crowd echoed back, "Christ is risen, indeed!" Immediately the hymns changed to songs of joy, praise, and exaltation. The congregation rushed into the church, worshiping God in loud voices. The resurrection of Jesus Christ from the dead had given the world its first and final hope.

Not since God laid the foundations of the world had anyone come back from the other side with a message of victory. The resurrection of Jesus Christ flung open the coffin lid, broke down the door to the mausoleum, and forever changed the view from the bottom of the grave. No longer did it make any difference if the ground was frozen, because Jesus Christ had brought the hope of an eternal spring. He has given us the victory! Fear has been defeated. Easter has come.

FACING OUR FEAR

In the last twenty years our world has shifted its philosophical perspective on spirituality. Earlier, many scholars doubted the existence of any spiritual reality. The logical positivists declared, "All you get is what you see." Then drug usage, psychedelics, and the discovery of how indecisive science can be changed the view of people on the street. And scholars started affirming that there was more to life than physical evidence could demonstrate. Love, trust, and hope couldn't be measured in a test tube. We started believing that all you see is *not* what you get. The scope of human experience was far vaster. Spiritual answers made a difference everywhere! Those changes altered how we face death today.

The place to start facing our fears of death is by examining the meaning of the death and resurrection of Jesus Christ. Jesus spoke with an extraordinary authority about His own death. With His apostles huddled around him, He said: "Do not let your heart be troubled; believe in God, believe also in Me. In My Father's house are many dwelling places; if it were not so, I would have told you; for I go to prepare a place for you. And if I go and prepare a place for you, I will come again, and receive you to Myself; that where I am, there you may be also" (John 14:1–3).

Before His staggeringly painful death, Jesus knew what was ahead. He proclaimed that He was preparing the way for His followers, breaking down death's door and leading them into an eternal future.

Previously, no one ever made such expansive statements. The world has observed great and magnificent leaders from Socrates to Alexander the Great down to the international leaders of our time like Churchill and Kennedy. They all died and not one came back. Only Jesus looked the final fear in the face and said, "I will come again, and receive you to Myself, that where I am, there you may be also." His remarkable prediction was fulfilled three days after His death as He stepped out of the tomb on Easter morning.

In addition, Jesus said, "You know the way where I am going" (John 14:4). The disciple named Thomas immediately responded that they had no idea where Jesus was going. Jesus' answer to Thomas's doubt remains forever the ultimate answer to his and our fears: "I am the way, and the truth, and the life; no one comes to the Father but through Me. If you had known Me, you would have known My Father also; from now on you know Him, and have seen Him" (John 14:6–7).

The answer to our fears isn't an idea or an explanation. *It is a person.* Through the dynamic of human personality, God has given us a pathway through the Person, Jesus Christ, to walk through our fears.

A BOLD CERTAINTY

Have you thought about the view from the bottom of the grave? You want to know how these facts from Scripture bear on your experience? How can you overcome your own fear of death?

Some years after writing his Gospel, John wrote a letter, following up many of the statements he had written earlier. By this time many of the people who had listened to Jesus teach and preach had died or were about to pass off the scene, including those whom Jesus had previously healed. The issues of death were even more pressing. Could they believe confidently in the meaning of the Resurrection? How would their faith change their apprehension about facing death?

John spoke directly to this problem: "And the testimony is this, that God has given us eternal life, and this life is in His Son. He who has the Son has the life; he who does not have the Son of God does not have the life. These things I have written to you who believe in the name of the Son of God, in order that you may know that you have eternal life" (1 John 5:11–13).

What John wrote can completely heal your fear of death. Consider carefully the following facts from this passage of Scripture.

Fact One: Eternal Life Is a Gift

You can't possibly do anything to change or affect the fact you will eventually die. If the matter was in your hands, you would have every reason to be terrified, but this isn't the case. *Nothing* is in your hands. Your inabilities aren't the issue.

The Creator of the universe is offering you this answer purely and totally as a gift, and you can receive the offer only as a gift. Every married person can remember the moment his spouse looked into his eyes and said tenderly, "I love you." Because of His unsurpassable love, our heavenly Father has said to us, "I love you," and offered the gift of eternal life. We only have to say yes.

Fact Two: The Gift Comes with the Giver

Far from an abstract idea, when we entered into a personal relationship with Jesus Christ, the gift came with the One giving His life. The apostle John said, "This life is in His Son. He who has the Son has the life." Our relationship with Christ conveys eternal life. When He promised to be the way, the truth, and the life, Jesus made Himself the bridge from time into eternity. John wrote to inform all people who have a relationship with Jesus that eternal life came with Him when He entered their lives.

For example, if I were trying to understand the relationship between time and space and Albert Einstein came to my house to explain the extraordinarily complex relationship, *insight would come with him.* Nothing I would have done or could do would change the fact that Einstein's remarkable mind offered understanding. In the same way, eternal life always comes with Jesus Christ.

Fact Three: The Gift Answers the Unknown

Many people are as concerned about the mysterious aspects of what lies beyond the grave as they are about dying itself. What they can't define remains frightening. While Jesus left many questions unanswered, He did bring some unique insights. Robert Wise discovered how powerful these could be when working with a child dying of cancer.

While ministering in California, the staff at St. Joseph's Hospital called to ask Robert to talk to a child named Maria who didn't speak English. They knew Robert spoke Spanish.

When Robert reached the hospital, he found five-year-old Maria, having lost her hair to chemotherapy, with small knots all over her body caused by tumors. As they talked, Robert quickly recognized the child was actually comforting her parents. The Mexican-Indian parents didn't speak English or Spanish well and cried continuously. They had never been in a church and didn't seem to know anything about the Christian faith. While he was concerned for the parents, Robert turned his attention to Maria, trying to help with her approaching death.

After the first visit, Maria began talking confidentially to Robert, telling him about the beautiful creatures she saw circulating above her in her dreams. Robert suggested that they might be angels and Maria was fascinated. They talked about the angels' protection and love. When Robert shared the Christian faith, Maria was completely receptive.

On his next visit, Maria was visibly weaker, but she was excited that a certain figure had entered her dreams. This wonderfully kind and loving man made Maria very happy. Robert suggested his name might be Jesus, and Maria should try calling him by that name if he returned in her next dreams.

The following day when Robert returned to the hospital, Maria could no longer sit up but beckoned him to come closer. She whispered in Robert's ear that Jesus had indeed come back to her dream. "The experience was wonderful," she said. "He told me that after this visit I don't have to come back anymore." Maria beamed and feebly hugged Robert.

Within a few minutes, Maria closed her eyes and peacefully drifted off to heaven. Whatever had been an unknown worry disappeared. She was now walking with Jesus into eternity.

To Robert Wise this was another example of the apostle John's testimony that God has given us eternal life through His Son, Jesus Christ.

Fact Four: The Gift Is for Today

Possibly one of the most remarkable aspects of this passage from 1 John is that the apostle wrote with a present-tense emphasis. John said he was writing "so that you may know that you have eternal life"—now. Eternal life is not only for the day we die; the gift is for this moment and remains continuously with us without end.

Through the centuries Christians have faced the greatest fears with Christ at their side and in their future; they have not run from their persecutors, from lions in the Coliseum, or from martyrdom at the stake. They knew God had already completely underwritten their future with promise. True, someday they would die, but it would only be a hop, skip, and jump into eternity. The physical pain they experienced in dying would be momentary; before them stretched an eternity of unbroken joy, causing the pain to vanish as quickly as if they had taken a breath.

ENDING OUR FEAR

John wanted believers to know they already had the gift of eternal life. For the Christian, fearing death is like fearing a frozen, slick highway when the temperature outside the window is ninety-plus degrees. It simply doesn't make any sense.

However, we've already observed that many phobias and fears are not based on fact. Under these circumstances, we need to practice some cognitive therapy and change our thinking. Here's a series of steps to help you do so. Use the space indicated to check your response.

_____*You Have Committed Your Life to Jesus Christ*

The answer to a fear of death begins by coming into a relationship with a person; not only believing what the Bible says is true but knowing Jesus personally. Once we have committed our lives to Jesus Christ, the door opens to receive His promises. You must first make Him the Supreme Friend of your life.

If you haven't done so, now is the moment to stop and ask Him into your life. You quietly bow your head and sincerely ask Jesus Christ to be part of everything you are. If you've never made that decision, *do it now.*

_____*Give Him Your Entire Life*

In addition to asking Jesus to be part of your life, you need to give Him every aspect of who you are. Here you surrender every aspect of your life—the negative as well as the positive.

If you've identified your own fears while reading this book, you need to ask Jesus to be part of those apprehensions. The

Scripture tells us perfect love casts out fear. As the love of Christ moves through your life, fear is pushed out. You need to ask Him in to the place where fear hides.

Stop and ask the love of Christ to start filling your fears with His promise and glory. Bow your head, close your eyes, and offer Him residence in every room in your world.

_____*Receive the Gift of Eternal Life*

At the same time that you asked Jesus Christ into your life, you received the gift of eternal life. Yet some sincere Christians don't know God has already given them this gift, because they have never stopped and said thank You. Accept this gift right now and your eternal life is secure.

If you made this decision, use the space below to write the date and time of your prayer. People tend to talk themselves out of the fact that the matter is settled. Having a date to remind you of when you made the decision to receive God's gift of eternal life will help you affirm that the matter is finished. Someday you will be with Him in heaven.

Date:_____

Does this decision make a difference? Millions and millions of people around the world give a resounding yes!

A FINAL THOUGHT

Your fears of death don't have the power to haunt you any longer, but you must learn to walk in confidence, trusting what God has done for you. When your fears of dying come to mind, you need to remind yourself that you are God's. You must trust and live by your faith.

Joe Harris had dug many graves, but following his conversation with Robert Wise, Joe put his cynicism behind him. In his own simple, straightforward manner, he asked for the confidence to know God had given him eternal life. Having prayed for an eternal hope, Joe went home that evening with new confidence. Eight years later Joe died and Robert held his funeral. As the casket was lowered into the grave, Robert knew the view from the bottom no longer made any difference to Mr. Harris. Joe now had a perspective from eternity.

FIFTEEN

Self-Control
to the Rescue

Everyone has those common, everyday kinds of fears. They pop up from the moment the sun rises until we go to bed at night. They aren't the sorts of worries we'd take to a psychiatrist or talk over with a counselor—they're too minuscule—but they still bother us. Slowly, inconspicuously, they erode our confidence in God's goodness.

Jack Brian and Harriet Ford certainly lived with such fears. Jack loved athletics, but he always played expecting to lose. Far from incapable, Jack had been a champion wrestler in high school and competed successfully in college. But he never played with confidence. Somewhere along the way, Jack picked up low self-esteem, assuming the kids in his neighborhood were all larger and stronger. His assessment carried over into the adult world where his tendency to give the other players more credit than was due set him up for failure. His mind-set kept him from achieving at the level of his capacities.

Harriet Ford's mother was well-known throughout the

community for her bizarre behavior. Consequently, Harriet grew up with a strong motivation to achieve and avoid the nonsense that motivated dear old Mom. Eventually, Harriet married and had a beautiful son. As the child grew, Harriet unintentionally instilled fear in her son. When a visitor appeared, Harriet would whisper in the child's ear, "Don't be afraid. He won't hurt you." The child got the message, "Watch out, because danger is coming through the door." Harriet taught her son to be afraid as she overcompensated for her mother's erratic behavior.

Do these people need help? Of course; they don't necessarily need therapy, but they could use some general guidance. And we could name an army of people with similar problems. Initial research, and common sense, indicates that the majority of New Yorkers were severely traumatized after the terrorist attack in September 2001. While many of these people continue methodically to go about their business every day, they could use an emotional shot in the arm to help them function without the constant fear of a bomb going off in the huge metropolitan area. For one reason or another, many people live continually under an umbrella of doubt. What can they do to find peace of mind?

Throughout this book Paul's instruction to Timothy has guided us: God did not give us a spirit of timidity (or fear) but of power and love and self-control (2 Tim. 1:7). In these last three chapters, we are going to look carefully at each of these gifts of grace to see how they can chase fear out of our lives. In this chapter, we will explore how inspired self-control can take care of the small apprehensions that bother us.

BE REALISTIC

During Stephen Arterburn's highly successful Women of Faith Conference in Philadelphia in November 2001, at which Lisa

Beamer spoke, he noticed a clear difference between how Lisa handled her grief over the loss of her husband, Todd, and how many other Americans faced their losses. The attack on September 11 tapped into the fear systems of millions of people. Whatever these people had once feared came to the top of the pile of all-encompassing dreads. Many people even stopped flying to such an extent it nearly bankrupted several airlines. Was the response realistic? No.

As a matter of record, airplanes are safer today than at any time since they were invented. More accidents happen within a five-mile radius of our own homes than anywhere else. We are still more secure flying than we are riding in our cars. Following September 2001, the airports' security checks became intense. So why were so many people fearful enough to quit flying altogether?

In the same way that Jack Brian and Harriet Ford didn't look at their lives accurately, Americans who gave up air travel weren't being realistic. Many people inevitably see the glass as half-empty and miss the good that is just as apparent. To stay on sound footing, people need to maintain a realistic perspective of the world around them.

Here are some ways to stay on an even keel.

1. Don't Overreact

We learn how to respond to life when we are children. If when we were young a bad experience rocked our world, we may have overreacted. Our response to the problem spawned a new habit, making us far too apprehensive when trouble starts. We grew up but our overreactions didn't change.

Most people have never analyzed their fears. They assume their extreme responses are typical. They need to sit down and examine those "little fears," and consider whether their reactions really suit the situation. They may need someone objective to help them with this, since their overreactions are a long-held habit.

Perhaps they can learn to say, "I'm overreacting. I need to settle down. There's nothing to be afraid of here."

2. Don't Ignore the Facts

We tend to lose sight of the fact we are part of a social system with an almost infinite number of safety valves built in to protect us. There are stoplights, warning signals, train-track crossing signs, policemen, and so on. The truth is, we are always more secure than we realize. When we ignore these important social securities, we see life through fear-filled eyes and expect the worst of every situation or encounter. The problem is we have failed to see how many ways we are kept safe in daily life. We have overlooked the facts.

Jack Brian overlooked the fact that he was athletically gifted, and Harriet Ford missed the point that her mother's strange behavior didn't have anything to do with Harriet's child. Periodically, people need a simple amount of data added. Self-control is required.

A salesman developed a fear of being hit by a train and began worrying that a locomotive would run him down on the highway. He shared this worry with Stephen Arterburn.

Stephen replied, "But trains need tracks to run on, don't they?"

The salesman blinked several times. "Yes," he answered with surprise, recognizing that trains can't run on a highway.

"You shouldn't have to worry about trains anymore," Stephen concluded.

The salesman's fear ended with that conversation. Facts made a difference.

3. Plan Ahead

Whenever possible, make the adjustments necessary to cover what you fear *ahead of time*. For example, if you worry about your car breaking down, spend the money to get a better car and keep it maintained. When the fears arise, you can access the fact that you keep the vehicle running like a top. Another technique we discussed earlier (paradoxical intention) would be to live every day as though your car will break down; when it eventually does break down, then you aren't disappointed because you expected it anyway. Afraid of burglars? Then buy a good security system. Sometimes our fears tell us to pay better attention; let's do it so we can quit fretting.

Stop for a moment and take a hard look at some of those nagging issues that keep bothering you. Your goal is to be more realistic and make adjustments that can save you problems. Use the space below to jot down how you might rearrange your circumstances to make those nagging little fears unnecessary.

Now, let's look in another direction.

PREPOSTEROUS PRESUPPOSITIONS

Is it possible some of your fears have arisen because of assumptions you've made but never examined? Presuppositions are ideas we've absorbed into our bloodstream without thinking about them or examining their sources. We grow up listening to people talk, explain, and state opinions that we take as fact. With time, some of these ideas prove false and we discard them; others cling and distort our worldview.

For example, Jack Brian lived with the presupposition that competitors were more capable than he was, and Harriet Ford took for granted that her role was to be the sword-swinging family protector. Correct? Not at all.

You might be afraid of spiders and snakes. Are some of them poisonous? Definitely, but the dangerous ones are in the vast minority. Most are harmless and important to maintaining the balance of nature; they kill flies, mosquitoes, and other insects. Is that your presupposition when you see one of these many-legged arthropods or a long, slithering serpent gliding through the grass? Instead, your assumption may be that death is thirty seconds away.

A frequently overlooked fact is that these creatures are more concerned to get out of your way than you are to get away from them. Does that make any difference to the fear-filled person? No, not at that moment. His presuppositions have already dictated his reaction.

Until we have explored our hypotheses about what scares us, fears control our lives. We have to face them and exercise some self-control in order to diminish the panic they create. Here are a couple of ways to open the blinds and let some light in.

Sit down and identify the issues that make you a worrier. Look at your fears carefully and examine the presuppositions behind them. You may be surprised to discover these apprehensions are based on ideas you've taken for granted. Are they really true? Are you really in the danger you suppose you are?

In the space below, list some of the presuppositions supporting your worries. Get in touch with what you've failed to consider in the past.

Next, carry your fears to their extreme conclusion: describe what would happen if the worst occurred. What would you do?

"Wait," you demand. "What if the worst alternative was getting killed? What then?"

In chapter 14 we covered facing the fear of death. Every Christian has his greatest hope in the world ahead. If you die, Jesus Christ has already opened the door to heaven. The worst turns into the best! Doesn't that help allay some of your fear?

The fact is, there already is an answer for every fear you have.

Take each overriding fear in your life and put it through the process described. Examine it for false presuppositions. Look at the worst outcome possible, and decide how to defuse it. Write each of these exercises in the space below so that you have a record you can return to when fear tries to take over once again. Self-control is your way to freedom.

Now let's look in yet another direction that may surprise you.

BAD RELIGION

Strange as it may seem, one of the reasons many people develop fear is because of what they have heard at church. Sometimes preachers offer only negative messages. We must uncover any possible ties between our fears and what we believe if we want to get free of our worries.

Harriet Ford's fears intensified when she joined a church that majored in spreading doubt. The sermons, the teachings, and the people were immersed in constant fear. The minister always closed his sermons with a veiled threat of what terrible results would occur when parishioners didn't do what he said. Classes detailed the stark realities of hell or the pending fiscal disaster waiting to send America into destitution. Participating in this congregation heightened Harriet's apprehensions to an unbearable level. Poor theology was robbing her of God's promised peace.

Some churches use guilt as a tool to convince and convict people. The negative twist turns the Christian gospel into a message of judgment and condemnation. People accepting this approach may walk out of a worship service saying, "It never felt so good to feel so bad." Sounds contradictory, doesn't it?

This mind-set was never a part of God's plan. God's gift wasn't fear or depression but power, love, and self-control, as Paul told Timothy.

Some churches also teach a skewed view of the will of God, as if it is a one-shot opportunity—make a foolhardy choice and forever miss God's plan for your life. Leaders teach young people that they have to find that one spouse God created for them or be miserable forever. Consequently, youth live with a constant fear of making a big mistake. The problem is bad theology.

In contrast, the Scriptures only tell us not to be unequally yoked with an unbeliever. We can marry any person we want who is a genuine Christian. The truth is there are many people we can happily marry and it is quite acceptable to God. And we have a choice to either get married or stay single (1 Cor. 7:25–40). The decision is up to us.

The same kind of teaching is often extended to the jobs people have. The implication is that God *really* smiles most favorably on full-time Christian employment. Being a pastor, a teacher, a missionary, or in any form of religious employment represents ultimate compliance with God's will. Everyone else's job is second best. The result is that many fine young people spend years with a quiet, unexamined fear they are in the wrong careers and not truly pleasing God.

Yet Paul practiced making tents as a way to put bread on the table as he ministered to the early Christians. His message was: being honest, diligent, and faithful as an employee as we make our witness for Christ fulfills God's call on our lives. Unless God intervenes, you don't have to change jobs to be in the center of His will.

LITTLE THINGS CAN MEAN A LOT

These examples will help you think about how your own apprehensions might be a product of distorted teaching. Anytime you start opening your eyes to the possibility you have believed the wrong ideas, the thought is more than a little threatening.

But wait a minute!

We have to shift through our ideas and disregard the bad ones throughout our lives. We do it at work, at home, with friends, and occasionally we need to do the same thing at church. Far from being unfaithful, we are practicing self-control when we rethink our assumptions about spiritual truths.

Use the space below to sort out some of what you have heard at church that troubles you. Then use your Bible to examine such thoughts to see if they are based on truth. Perhaps you might ask a trusted mentor to help you.

Sometimes our ideas just need fine-tuning. A small adjustment can make an enormous difference. Consider a ship traveling to Japan. A slight variation of a couple of degrees on the ship's compass wouldn't make much difference in leaving the harbor. If left unchecked, though, the variation would take the ship to Australia, not to Japan!

Earlier in this chapter we mentioned Todd Beamer, who on September 11 uttered the infamous words, "Let's roll." He and some courageous travelers did what they could to prevent terrorists from crashing their plane into another building or monument and causing even more deaths. All of them are to be admired for facing their fears and acting in spite of them.

In your journey through life you have a terrorist on board, Satan, who wants nothing better than for you to crash and burn. But every day God invites you to control your fears and utters to you, "Let's roll."

SIXTEEN

Turning Points
Toward Power

Few biblical heroes struggled with as many fearful experiences as Joseph did. In Genesis, the story of this extremely bright, talented young man unfolds, making clear that Joseph was the favorite of Jacob, his father. Of course, Joseph's brothers were more than a little irritated with his arrogant attitude. They finally became so angry they contemplated killing Joseph. From that point forward, Joseph's life was a roller coaster of good and evil experiences, providing him with many reasons to be afraid. But in the end, when Joseph had been elevated to the rank of a prince of Egypt and his decisions meant the survival of thousands of people who faced starvation, his terrified but needy brothers were forced to seek his help. They knew Joseph had the power and the position to execute them. Fear was now the brothers' problem.

Joseph's response to his family was remarkably inspired. It's an important message for our time as well: "You meant evil against me, but God meant it for good in order to bring about this present result, to preserve many people alive" (Gen. 50:20). What the brothers intended for harm became God's opportunity for good! His power overruled their bad intentions.

Like the startling conclusion of an O. Henry short story, everything in Joseph's life turned out different from what his attackers intended. Each of us struggles to believe such an unexpected switch could happen in our own lives—we tend to believe Joseph is an exception to the rule. The truth is Joseph was basically a faithful man who didn't veer from what God called him to be and to do. The point of the stories in Joseph's life is to teach people who remain steadfast that they will be delivered. The same is true for anyone struggling with fear today.

Your surprise endings are not the product of only working harder but of being tenacious in your faith, exercising the power God gave you (2 Tim. 1:7). In order to encourage you to let faith help you out of the pits created by your apprehensions, look at several stories of faith that reflect the same discovery Joseph made about God's power to use evil for His highest purposes.

In this chapter, we want to encourage you. Previous chapters have given you assignments and tasks that required emotion and effort. The task of facing fear may have proved more difficult than you anticipated. We want you to know your effort isn't in vain. God wants to give you the gift of power, the capacity to overcome. You are creating a new tomorrow for yourself. Don't worry. Following are examples of people who didn't give up.

TURNING LOSS INTO LIBERTY

We often review the lives of our heroes with such a quick sweep that we miss the deeper, more painful moments. As one stands at the base of the awesome Lincoln Memorial in Washington, D.C., staring up at the magnificent figure of Lincoln looking out peacefully across the Reflecting Pool, it is not easy to detect the grief and distress lurking in the shadows. The truth is Lincoln had to climb mountains of affliction before anyone recognized his greatness. Nowhere was the struggle more evident than with his first love.

In the summer of 1835, Abe Lincoln was a member of the Illinois legislature and people saw him as a man with a bright future. A young woman caught Lincoln's eye. Ann Rutledge was a red-haired beauty whom Lincoln found delightful. He would ride over to chat with her at the farm where she worked. They spent time talking about their futures, contemplating the possibility of Ann's attending the Jacksonville Female Academy while Abe attended the Illinois Center. A promising tomorrow lay ahead for both of them. Abe envisioned them as man and wife forever.

As August drew to a close and the corn ripened, the chills and fever of malaria spread across the valley. Lincoln struggled with his own aches and pains, having to take a bitter medicine made of Peruvian bark and boneset tea. So many died, Abe even had to help make caskets. Then word came that Ann Rutledge had taken ill.

Lincoln rushed to her home on the Sand Ridge farm only to find Ann near death. In the log cabin with dim shades of light settling over Ann's face, Abe sat alone, watching his love's life drain away. After the funeral in the Concord burying ground, Lincoln refused to be consoled. For hours on end, he sat by himself, consumed by his grief.

A week after the burial, a friend saw Lincoln rambling through the woods along the Sangamon River almost incoherent, mumbling sentences no one could understand. As the weeks of autumn passed, Lincoln continued to spend time alone, lost in his pain. He was heard to say, "I can't bear to think of her out there alone." Grief had devoured him.[1]

With time, Abe Lincoln reestablished order in his life, but he had become a changed man. The transformation had come at a cost Lincoln never spoke of.

Fear? Loss? Grief? All those emotions and more haunted Lincoln, but his faith sustained him. His pain made him incredibly strong. He could endure the fury of the enormous Union losses at Gettysburg and other Civil War battlefields, as well as in his own family, because of what he had first endured in the woods of Illinois. Abraham's faith and the power he received from it carried him forward. Dealing with his own personal loss equipped Lincoln to save the nation.

Many American presidents have faced similar crises that uniquely prepared them for their tasks in office. During the war with terrorists and the al-Qaeda network, observers pointed to the tenacious resolve of President George W. Bush, which reflected Bush's coming to grips with his own emotional pain and fears.

Early in his adult life, George W. Bush struggled with an alcohol problem. Finally, after a harsh conversation with his wife, Laura, George realized he had to come to grips with the addiction threatening to defeat him. In his subsequent search for sobriety, Bush recognized his need for a higher power and accepted Christ as his Savior. He made the decision to face his fears and stop the problem.

As president, he draws on the same strength he found in those lonely days of personal struggle to fight an enemy threatening the future of the entire United States. Again, Christian faith made the difference.

In both of these cases, what was meant for evil—a loved one's death and addiction to alcohol—became a tool for good. Having to face what frightens us can be as difficult as it was for Lincoln or Bush. Yet, as in their cases, we will find that facing fears uniquely equips us for the future and expresses God's power to turn evil to good.

Is this still true when our pit is emotional illness?

Turning Depression into Determination

Possibly you have struggled for many years with fear, and depression has been the only result. Consequently, you wonder whether it is worth the effort to keep fighting to become an emotionally healthy person. Before you throw in the towel, consider an experience out of Dr. Paul Meier's practice.

Dan Hanson, a Lutheran pastor, and his wife, Maria, lived in Sweden with their five children. The problem started when Maria began to develop severe anxiety. As her illness progressed, Maria became fearful of leaving the house and eventually would not leave even her bedroom. Maria's agoraphobia kept her from going to church or working, but the problem developed further. Dan was left with the job of caring for the children.

As her anxiety increased, Maria experienced swelling in her cranial area. Although a wide range of neurologists and psychiatrists examined her, no one knew what to do. Eventually, Maria was placed in a hospital where she experienced periods of hibernation, sleeping for as long as several months at a time. Finally, the doctors had no other advice for Dan Hanson except that he commit Maria to a mental hospital for the rest of her life.

At this point Dan Hanson read *Happiness Is a Choice* and decided to call around the world to reach author Dr. Paul Meier. Would Paul consider treating Maria? After considering her case, Paul said he would care for her if Reverend Hanson could bring her to Dallas. Dan immediately got Maria on an airplane.

Paul used the Gestalt techniques we've described and other therapies with a biblical approach and helped Maria get in touch with the past. Maria admitted she had experienced a variety of abuses when she was a child. Flashbacks of abuse had triggered her agoraphobia attacks. Maria began to recognize her need to wrestle with these past fears. She started talking about her repressed pain and finally came to the place where she could begin to forgive her abusers.

During therapy, Paul discovered that Maria's parents had never given her a birthday party. So the staff threw a huge party and completely overwhelmed Maria with their love and affection. Paul even bought her a teddy bear. Maria wept because she had never experienced love from an authority figure in her life. Maria Hanson went home a whole person.

Newspapers across Sweden reported her story because she seemed to have experienced a miracle cure in America. As Maria talked with her Swedish doctors, they expressed a desire for Paul to teach them this marvelous Christian approach to therapy. Paul went to Sweden and trained more than three hundred doctors, therapists, and pastors in how they could use his various approaches. Many of the trainees became Christians.

The medical response was so significant that Maria has become an instrumental leader in the Christian psychology movement in Sweden through public speaking, leading Bible studies on psychological issues, writing articles, and even speaking to the Swedish government about these needs in the country. What began as Maria's illness became a healing crusade that affected an entire country.

What obviously began as an evil assault on this woman's mind was turned into God's hope for tomorrow because of Maria's tenacity and God's power. Could that be true in your life? Is it possible your fears might be the prelude to a great victory? No one knows except you as you remain determined to face your fears with God's help. You can turn humiliation into hope.

TURNING HUMILIATION INTO HOPE

The first time Robert Wise saw Cherie Carver was at the end of a worship service after she had been attending his church for several weeks. The congregation had become such a booming fellowship that it was hard for Robert to meet the many people who came for the first time each week. As Cherie shook his hand at the back door, she said quietly, "I'd like to talk to you when you have a few moments."

"Sure," Robert said. "How about this Tuesday for lunch?"

They set a time and Robert met Cherie at a restaurant near the church. He often practiced evangelism by meeting people over a sandwich and talking about the Christian faith. Each week new members were added to the church from these times of sharing and praying together. His meeting with Cherie proved significant.

"I had never been in a church except at a funeral or a wedding," Cherie began, "but I was driving down the street several weeks ago when I saw this enormous parking lot crammed with automobiles. I had no idea what that many people were doing at a gathering on a Sunday morning, so I stopped to see."

Cherie described slipping into the back door of the church and being greeted so cheerfully and enthusiastically that she stayed for worship. The morning message touched her. Not able to grasp everything she heard, Cherie knew she had to come back. She had not missed a Sunday since her first visit.

"And what are you asking me?" Robert inquired.

"I want to become a Christian," Cherie answered. "I've heard enough to know this is where I want to spend the rest of my life! Can I join?"

Robert was taken aback because usually he was the one pushing the message. As they talked further, Cherie made it clear she wanted her life to change. Later, Robert baptized her and she became an enthusiastic part of the congregation. Robert made sure Cherie got into a small group and turned his attention to other inquirers, but several months later Cherie returned to his office. This time she looked troubled and broken.

"I didn't tell you everything," Cherie began apologetically. "I thought my problem would simply disappear when I joined the church . . . but it hasn't." Tears welled up in her eyes. "I can't get my problem off my mind and I don't think I can go on being a Christian." Over the next thirty minutes Cherie told a frightening story of a fear stuck in her heart like a spear.

Highly intelligent and skilled, she had been an important part of a local computer company. Cherie had heard that many of the men lived rough lives, but she didn't expect their behavior to bother her. One evening she worked late, finishing the assignment for the day. Hearing a noise, Cherie turned from her computer to discover three of the top executives standing in her office. Looking glazed and bleary-eyed, they were obviously drunk or high.

"Want to fool around?" one of the vice presidents asked in slurred syllables.

Before Cherie knew what was happening, the men dragged her out from behind her desk and one of them assaulted her. No amount of screaming, slugging, and fighting could stop the rape. As the humiliation came to an end, one of the men leaned down in her face and warned Cherie that if she told anyone, they would kill her.

The terror of that moment had lurked in the back of Cherie's mind for several years. She was convinced the men had the capacity to kill her. Even though Cherie quit working for the company, her fear wouldn't go away. The memory of the horror had wrecked her life. When becoming a Christian and joining a church didn't erase her terror, she wondered what in the world she could do next.

Robert began working with Cherie therapeutically, helping her sort out her feelings so she could discover how to defuse her fears. She practiced the Gestalt technique of talking to a chair, pretending the man who had attacked her was sitting there.

Cherie's struggle was intense. It took several months of hard work to conquer the fear that had haunted her for so long. She grieved, cried, thought, prayed, and finally came to the place where she could release what had happened to her. Her pain began to subside.

A year later she told Robert, "I've been thinking about what I've lived through. Probably there are many women who have had to live through similar agony."

"Yes," Robert agreed, "unfortunately, your experience has happened in different ways to many people. Most of them never face the problem until it becomes too overwhelming."

Cherie answered, "I've been thinking about the help they need, and I want to be available to make a difference if I can." She looked up with tears in her eyes. "Robert, would you help me become a minister?"

Cherie went to a seminary and in three years completed the graduate training. Then Robert hired her to be the minister of singles in his church, and Cherie later married a minister. Today she and her husband jointly serve a congregation not far from where Robert lives. She is helping men and women recover from painful attacks.

An easy journey? No, it was one of the hardest in the world, but Cherie is helping other strugglers find a new path—to discover God's power to turn harm into opportunity for extraordinary good. If you are struggling to keep working at facing your fears, Cherie would smile and assure you it's worth every ounce of energy.

YOUR SURPRISE ENDING

As you consider your alternatives, don't ever forget the basic lesson Joseph gave the world. While hard work is extremely important, the final answer for any situation in our lives comes simply from our faithfulness!

Fear always feels like it has the strength of a nuclear attack. It always will! In contrast, faith is an unseen and seldom-felt trust in God's capacity to lead us forward. Joseph went from the pit to Potiphar's house and to prison before he ended up in the palace. He had plenty of time to cower in the darkness, but he remained confident God would eventually reinstate him—and He did. Many, many times, Joseph's emotions must have run away like an avalanche. In the end, faith pulled Joseph out of despair and set him on firm ground.

You can make the same journey!

Your faith can pull you out of any emotional pit and send you to God's palace. *God has given you this power* (remember 2 Timothy 1:7). That's how you write your surprise ending to your life's story.

SEVENTEEN

The Greatest
of These—Love

On April 19, 1995, Cathy Wilburn and her daughter, Edye Smith, left for work at Oklahoma City's Internal Revenue Service office building as they did every morning of the week. Edye placed Chase and Colton, her two- and three-year-old sons, in the child-care center up the street from the offices where she and Cathy worked. Another working day had started as usual.

At 9:01 an overwhelming boom shook the street and the IRS building trembled. A block away a giant cloud of smoke shot up in the air. Countless pieces of fragmented glass showered down on the sidewalks. The Murrah Building had just been bombed.

Cathy and Edye ran up the street to the child-care center— which was located in the Murrah Building. When they reached the front of the multistoried structure, they saw only the smoking wreckage of a huge building blown to pieces. Somewhere beneath the rubble of concrete and twisted steel were those two little boys.

Throughout the rest of the day, the search for survivors went on as firemen attempted to overturn the huge pieces of crumbled cement. Cathy and Edye were sent to a local hospital, and they hoped that the boys would soon arrive in an ambulance. But neither boy appeared. Finally, Cathy's policeman son, Danny Coss, arrived at the hospital, and they asked him to find out what had happened to the boys. By the middle of the afternoon, Danny had discovered the truth. Chase and Colton had died in the blast.

Cathy Wilburn and Edye Smith were devastated beyond what words could ever express. Their most precious gifts had been whisked away in a matter of seconds. How could Cathy and Edye go on?

In the last two chapters, we have explored a portion of Paul's letter to Timothy helping us overcome similar terrible fears. Let's look at it once again: "For God has not given us a spirit of timidity, but of power and love and discipline [or self-control]." In this final chapter we turn now to the most powerful promise Paul offered people like Cathy and Edye to help in their recovery . . . love!

Is it possible to overcome pain through love? Today Cathy Wilburn and Edye Smith would tell you it is.

READY FOR THE BEST?

As amazing and overwhelming as it may sound, love does have the capacity to change our perspectives so radically that we can set aside our worst fears. Even the results of tragedy and death can eventually be swallowed by the power of love.

The Bible reminds us: "Beloved, do not be surprised at the fiery ordeal among you, which comes upon you for your testing, as though some strange thing were happening to you; but to the degree that you share the sufferings of Christ, keep on rejoicing; so that also at the revelation of His glory, you may rejoice with exultation" (1 Peter 4:12–13). From Genesis to the book of Revelation, we read story after story of struggle. Whether we accept the fact or not, evil is always ready to put painful obstacles in our path.

Cathy and Edye had done nothing to deserve what transpired. Quite to the contrary, they had lived good Christian lives, but as predictably as is the rising of the sun every morning, evil struck and pain followed. Chase and Colton died.

The "fiery ordeal" Peter mentioned literally means "a burning." Peter was describing our struggle as a journey through fire, much like a smelting process that removes foreign particles from gold. Under intense heat, impurities rise to the top of the molten gold and are skimmed off. In an identical way, the apostle Peter reminds the Cathys and Edyes of this world that God didn't create those terrible disasters, but He will use the burning fires to purify their lives and finally produce gold . . . even when tragedy is unavoidable.

LOVE CHANGES THINGS

Having spent hours with Cathy Wilburn, Dr. Robert Wise knows the unspeakable depth of the pain those little boys' deaths caused their grandmother and mom. Brokenness wrenched their souls, but through the lonely nights, love did its work. God's profound affection and vigilance changed them.

Love modified their focus.

While fear may be justified and necessary at the moment a calamity strikes, it is still a radical form of self-centeredness. Hit your thumb with a hammer, and what happens? You don't smile and wish everyone around the world your best. You scream and hold your hand as if it is the center of the globe. At that moment nothing in the entire world matters as much as your thumb. Is this a normal response? Sure. But it's important to recognize how pain works in any of us. We become absolutely and totally concerned about *ourselves*. Fear operates in exactly the same way.

On the other hand, love turns our attention in another direction. Love allows us to look above and beyond our own pain and fear. Changing perspective can set us free from apprehension. In this way, love casts out fear because it refocuses our attention.

LOVING YOUR ENEMIES

In the Sermon on the Mount, Jesus gave a remarkable commandment that has everything to do with removing fear. He said, "Love your enemies and pray for those who persecute you" (Matt. 5:44). Jesus said that we are to care about the very people causing us to have fear. Is such a thing possible?

After Cathy and Edye had buried Chase and Colton, Cathy had a burning need to know the full truth about what happened in the Oklahoma City bombing. She set out to uncover every piece of evidence the government had not explained or fully clarified. The search sent her all over the United States, following the trail of Timothy McVeigh and Terry Nichols, trying to uncover details about what kind of hate created a bomb with the capacity to kill 169 people. During her journey, Cathy met many eccentric people as well as perpetrators in the explosion who had killed her grandchildren. But behind the scenes love was working.

During the Nichols trial in Denver, Cathy noticed Terry

Nichols's mother standing alone as people came and went from the courtroom. The little woman looked frightened, lonely, and very much in need of a friend. Cathy thought about this strange dilemma. The mother of one of the men responsible for her grandchildren's death, desperately needed someone to put her arms around her and shield her from the onslaught of the media and the hostile observers at the trial. Cathy stepped forward.

During the following days, Cathy Wilburn became friends with Terry Nichols's mother as well as his sister, Susan. Cathy began to genuinely care about these women, wanting the best for them. A love beyond any affection Cathy had ever known emerged. To her amazement, Cathy Wilburn found herself offering her home and resources to help this family. In the weeks that followed, the Nichols family stayed with her and received the emotional support Cathy offered.

Does this happen often? Certainly not by accident! It is a gift. God placed a gift of love in Cathy's heart. She is certainly a loving person, but her feelings for this family were extraordinary. The gift of unconditional love was God's grace and offer to Cathy.

There's More

Up to this point, we've been talking about love as an attitude we choose to have, but God has more to say about why love is so powerful. Love is also a gift. God can give us His gift of love, enabling us to experience change in ways we wouldn't have dreamed possible.

In 1 Corinthians 12, Paul talked about the gifts God bestows on the church. In the last verse of that chapter, he told us to seek the "greater gifts." One of the most extraordinary chapters in the Bible follows; here Paul described what the Greeks called *agape* love, the highest form of devotion in this world. First Corinthians

13 defines this adoration as being patient, kind, not jealous or boastful. This form of caring believes, hopes, bears, and endures all things with an unending commitment. Such a supreme form of love naturally pushes out fear.

Because Paul described *agape* love as a gift, he suggested God will give love to us in the same way that He gives His other gifts such as joy, peace, patience, kindness, as well as the ability to teach, preach, and bring people to wholeness. He bestows them on us.

How does anyone receive such a gift with the capacity to drive fear out of his life? The apostle John described it: "Beloved, let us love one another, for love is from God; and everyone who loves is born of God and knows God" (1 John 4:7). As you live your life daily in and through Jesus Christ, this gift of love emerges. Cathy Wilburn's ability to love Terry Nichols's family was a product of her life in Christ.

Look at an interesting passage in the New English Bible of the New Testament. First Peter 1:22 says, "Now that by obedience to the truth you have purified your souls until you feel sincere affection [love] towards your brother Christians, love one another whole-heartedly with all your strength." Peter was urging people who love each other to love each other? Make sense? Not completely, unless you recognize that the words for love in this passage actually come from two different Greek words. The first reference to love here, sincere affection, is *philadelphian,* which is the Greek word for caring about the people we like because we have mutual interests. However, Peter urged us to go on and strive to obtain another kind of love, *agape* love, which is a love for people we don't know and might even perceive to be our enemies.

Peter was telling us to start with the natural affection we feel for people we have reason to care about, then to keep on loving and moving toward a godly love that sees beyond differences and sins. Is it possible? Cathy Wilburn demonstrated it is. Powerful stuff? You bet, and it will set your life free from fear.

AND WHAT ABOUT YOU?

Do you love people? Some people automatically answer with a resounding yes, while others would have to admit it is a struggle. For many people, the older they get, the more difficult it becomes to love because of their many disappointments. So many evil people exist in the world that every adult has faced pain someone else has inflicted. But the damage other people have done to us never negates the command to love our enemies. If we give in to pain, we remain chained to fear. It's that simple.

So, do you love people? Can you turn vengeance for evil actions over to God and continue to love people in spite of their human frailties?

The apostle Peter suggested we start with sincere affection toward our fellow Christians, the people we can naturally care about, and build from there. That's a good place for you to start. How could you care more consistently for the people you know? Give it some careful thought. Then push on.

Would you like to press on toward obtaining the ability to love with the wonderful *agape* love both Peter and Paul described? Wouldn't it be a tremendous experience to be able to love everyone with the unconditional totality of an all-accepting love that would also banish your fear? It begins with a decision. The more unloved you were growing up, the harder it will be, but with the help of God and safe people, you can do it!

At this point, you will want to bow your head and fervently pray. Ask God to bless you with the gift that will cast out all fear.

In turn, tell Him you have decided to live your life through Jesus Christ as you wait for this gift to emerge.

A Final Thought

Throughout this book, and particularly in these last three chapters, we have been exploring how Paul's advice to Timothy can help diminish our fear. Paul stated that God has given us a gift of power, self-control, and love. As Paul ended the "love chapter," 1 Corinthians 13, he wrote, "But now abide faith, hope, love, these three; but the greatest of these is love."

Love equips us to do the right thing when it must be done. By its very nature love gives us an ability to exceed our fears and lifts us to a higher plane. In that way love pushes our fears aside.

The end of all the Gospel stories offers us the supreme example of how effective love is in casting out fear. On the night before His execution, Jesus retreated to the Garden of Gethsemane to pray for a reprieve from the terrible agony placed before Him. Jesus was frightened of the pain to the point of producing sweat that "became like drops of blood" (Luke 22:44). Like every Jew, He had seen men die on a cross, bathed in sweat and drenched in blood as life slowly, slowly drained out of their bodies. Jesus understood that death came as a slow suffocation. Regardless of the loftiness or grandeur of his cause, anyone would run from the prospects of such a death.

Nevertheless, the rest of the story took a decisive turn as Jesus made the decision that drove out fear: "Yet not My will," He prayed, "but Thine be done" (Luke 22:42). Surrender to God meant the difference between paralyzing fear and freedom to save the world. Evidence of the completeness of Jesus' love rings out in some of His last words: "Father, forgive them; for they do not know what they are doing" (Luke 23:34).

Love cast out His fears and it will cast out yours. You can count on it. That's the promise of God. From the first century down to this very hour, millions of believers have demonstrated we are meant to be the overcomers. Now it is your turn.

Acknowledgments

I (Dr. Paul Meier) would like to express my sincere appreciation for psychiatrist David Larson's prayer support throughout this project. David has been my close friend, my "cheerleader," and my prayer partner since we studied under Dr. Bill Wilson together at Duke University in the 1970s. Sixty percent of medical schools in America have courses on spirituality designed by my fellow confessor, Dr. David Larson, who died suddenly of a heart attack on March 5, 2002. I'll see you in heaven, buddy!

—Paul Meier, M.D.

APPENDIX A

Phobias[1]

Fear of	Condition
Air	Aerophobia
Aloneness	Autophobia, Eremophobia, Monophobia
Animals	Zoophobia
Anything new	Kainophobia, Neophobia
Bacilli	Bacillophobia
Bad men	Pavor Sceleris, Scelerophobia
Barren space	Cenophobia, Kenophobia
Bearing a deformed child	Teratophobia
Bees	Apiphobia, Melissophobia
Being buried alive	Taphephobia
Being enclosed	Clithrophobia
Being looked at	Scopophobia
Being touched	Haphephobia
Birds	Ornithophobia
Blood	Hematophobia, Hemophobia

Blushing	Ereuthrophobia, Erythrophobia
Brain disease	Meningitophobia
Bridges	Gephyrophobia
Burglars	Scelerophobia
Cats	Ailurophobia, Galeophobia, Gatophobia
Change	Kainophobia, Kainotophobia, Neophobia
Childbirth	Maieusiophobia
Choking	Anginophobia, Pnigophobia
Churches	Ecclesiaphobia
Cold	Cheimaphobia, Psychrophobia
Color	Chromatophobia, Chromophobia
Comet	Cometophobia
Confinement	Claustrophobia
Corpses	Necrophobia
Crossing streets	Dromophobia
Crowds	Demophobia, Ochlophobia Achlophobia
Dampness	Hygrophobia
Darkness	Nyctophobia, Scotophobia
Dawn	Eosophobia
Daylight	Phengophobia
Death	Thanatophobia
Defecation	Rhypophobia
Definite disease	Monopathophobia
Deformity	Dysmorphophobia
Demons	Demonophobia, Demonomania, Entheomania

Dentists	Detalphobia
Depth	Bathophobia
Devil, the	Demonophobia, Satanophobia
Dirt	Mysophobia, Rupophobia
Disease	Nosophobia, Pathophobia
Dogs	Cynophobia
Dolls	Phediophobia
Driving	Amaxophobia
Dust	Amathophobia
Eating	Pagophobia
Electricity	Electrophobia
Emptiness	Kenophobia
Everything	Panphobia, Panophobia, Pantophobia
Examinations (Tests)	Examination Phobia
Excrement	Coprophobia
Eyes	Ommatophobia
Failure	Kakorrhaphiophobia
Fatigue	Kopophobia
Fearing	Phobophobia
Feathers	Pteronophobia
Female genitals	Eurotophobia
Fever	Fibriphobia, Pyrexeophobia
Filth	Mysophobia, Rupophobia
Filth, personal	Automysophobia
Fire	Pyrophobia
Fish	Icthyophobia
Floods	Antlophobia

Flying	Aerophobia
Fog	Homichlophobia
Food	Cibophobia, Sitophobia
Forest	Hylophobia
Frogs	Batrachophobia
Functioning	Ergasiophobia
Germs	Mikrophobia
Ghosts	Phasmophobia
Girls	Parthenophobia
Glass	Crystallophobia, Hyelophobia
God	Theophobia
Gravity	Barophobia
Hair	Trichopathophobia
Heat	Thermophobia
Height	Acrophobia, Hyposophobia
Hell	Hadephobia, Stygiophobia
Heredity	Patroiophobia
High objects	Batophobia
Houses	Domatophobia, Oikophobia
Ideas	Ideophobia
Infinity	Apeirophobia
Injury	Traumatophobia
Innovation	Neophobia
Insanity	Lyssophobia, Maniaphobia
Insects	Acarophobia, Entomophobia
Jealousy	Zelophobia
Justice	Dikephobia
Knives	Aichmophobia

Large objects	Megalophobia
Light	Photophobia
Lightning	Astraphobia
Machinery	Mechanophobia
Man	Androphobia
Many things	Polyphobia
Marriage	Gamophobia
Materialism	Hylephobia
Medicine	Pharmacophobia
Metals	Metallophobia
Meteors	Meteorophobia
Mice	Murophobia
Mirrors	Eisoptrophobia, Spectrophobia
Missiles	Ballistophobia
Moisture	Hygrophobia
Money	Chrematophobia
Motion	Kinesophobia
Myths	Mythophobia
Naked bodies	Gymnophobia
Name	Onomatophobia
Needles	Belonephobia, Trypanophobia
Night	Noctiphobia, Myctophobia
Northern lights	Auroraphobia
Novelty	Kainophobia, Kainolophobia
Ocean	Thalassophobia
Odor	Bromidrosiphobia
Open space	Agoraphobia
Pain	Algophobia, Odynophobia

Parasites	Parasitophobia
People	Anthropophobia
Pleasure	Hedonophobia
Poison	Iophobia, Toxicophobia
Poverty	Peniaphobia
Precipices	Cremnophobia
Punishment	Poinephobia
Rabies	Cynophobia, Lyssophobia
Railroads or trains	Siderodromophobia
Rain	Qmbrophobia
Rectum	Proctophobia
Red	Erythrophobia
Reptiles	Herpetophobia
Responsibility	Hypengyophobia
Ridicule	Categelophobia
Rivers	Potamophobia
Robbers	Harpaxophobia
Rods	Rhabdophobia
Ruin	Atephobia
Sacred things	Hierophobia
Scabies	Scabiophobia
School	School Phobia
Scratches	Amychophobia
Seas	Thalassophobia
Self	Autophobia
Semen	Spermatophobia
Sexual intercourse	Coitophobia
Shock	Hormephobia

Sin	Hamartophobia
Sinning	Peccatiphobia
Sitting	Thaasophobia
Skin disease	Dermatosiophobia
Skin lesions	Dermatophobia
Skins of animals	Doraphobia
Sleep	Hypnophobia
Small objects	Microphobia, Microbiophobia
Smothering	Pnigerophobia
Snakes	Ophidiophobia
Snow	Chionphobia
Solitude	Eremophobia
Sounds	Acousticophobia
Sourness	Acerophobia
Speaking	Laliophobia
Speaking aloud	Phonophobia
Speaking, public	Topophobia
Spiders	Arachnaphobia
Stairs	Climacophobia
Standing up	Stasiphobia
Standing up and walking	Stasibasiphobia
Stars	Siderophobia
Stealing	Kleptophobia
Stillness	Eremiophobia
Stories	Mythophobia
Strangers	Xenophobia
Streets	Agyiophobia
Sunlight	Heliophobia

Symbolism	Symbolophobia
Syphilis	Syphilophobia
Talking	Laliophobia
Tapeworms	Taeniophobia
Taste	Geumaphobia
Teeth	Odontophobia
Thinking	Phronemophobia
Thunder	Astraphobia, Brontophobia
Time	Chronophobia
Travel	Hodophobia
Trembling	Tremophobia
Trichinosis	Trichinophobia
Tuberculosis	Phthisiophobia, Tuberculophobia
Vaccination	Vaccinophobia
Vehicles	Amaxophobia
Venereal Disease	Cypridophobia, Cypriphobia
Void	Kenophobia
Vomiting	Emetophobia
Walking	Basiphobia
Water	Aquaphobia, Hydrophobia
Weakness	Asthenophobia
Wind	Anemophobia
Women	Gynophobia, Horror Feminae
Words, hearing certain	Onomatophobia
Work	Ponophobia
Writing	Graphophobia

Appendix B

Books on Dreaming

You may want to explore the world of dreams further. We have found the following books to be helpful.

Cirlot, J. E. *Dictionary of Symbols*. New York: Philosophical Library, 1962.

Meier, Paul, and Robert L. Wise. *Windows of the Soul*. Nashville, Tenn.: Thomas Nelson, 1995.

Montague, Ullman, and Nan Zimmerman. *Working with Dreams*. New York: Dell, 1979.

Savory, Louis M., Patricia H. Berne, and Strephon Kaplan-Williams. *Dreams and Spiritual Growth: A Christian Approach to Dream Work*. New York: Paulist Press, 1984.

Notes

Chapter 8

1. Robin Pearson. "Phobias," *The Orange County Register,* Sunday, April 13, 1986. H section, p. 1.

2. "The Fight to Conquer Fear," *Newsweek,* April 23, 1984, pp. 66–68.

3. Ibid.

4. Ibid.

Chapter 10

1. Lloyd Lewis, *Myths after Lincoln* (New York: Grosset & Dunlap, 1957), p. 294.

2. Lous M. Savary; Patricia Berne; Strephon Kaplan-Williams. *Dreams and Spiritual Growth* (New York: Paulist Press, 1984) pp. 50–52.

Chapter 16

  1. Carl Sandburg. *Abraham Lincoln: The Prairie Years,* Vol. 1 (New York: Charles Scribner's Sons, 1926), p. 190.

Appendix A

  1. Adapted from: L. E. Hinsie and R. J. Campbell, *Psychiatric Dictionary,* 4th ed. (Fair Lawn, NJ: Oxford University Press, 1970).

About the Authors

Author of twenty-six published books, **Robert L. Wise, Ph.D.**, also writes for numerous magazines and journals, including *Christianity Today, Leadership*, and *The Christian Herald*. He is a bishop in the Communion of Evangelical Episcopal Churches. He collaborated on the national bestselling Millennium series, which includes *The Third Millennium, The Fourth Millennium*, and *Beyond the Millennium*, and is the author of *Be Not Afraid, Spiritual Abundance*, and the Sam and Vera Sloan Mystery series.

Nationally recognized psychiatrist and cofounder of New Life Clinics (1-800-NEW-LIFE), **Paul Meier, M.D.**, is cohost of the national radio program *New Life Live!* He is also the bestselling author or coauthor of more than fifty books, including *Love Is a Choice, Happiness Is a Choice, Windows of the Soul, Don't Let Jerks Get the Best of You*, and *Love Hunger*. Meier also collaborated on the bestselling Millennium series, which includes three futuristic novels, and *The Secret Code*.

Stephen Arterburn, M.Ed., is the creator of the Women of Faith Conferences. Since their inception in 1996, attendance at these conferences has exceeded two million women. He is also the founder of New Life Clinics, the largest Christian provider of counseling and treatment in the United States and Canada, and host of *New Life Live!*, a nationally syndicated live talk show aired on more than 120 outlets and at www.newlife.com. Arterburn is the bestselling author of more than forty books, including *Avoiding Mr. Wrong, The God of Second Chances, Every Man's Battle,* and *Flashpoints*. He can be reached at SArterburn@newlife.com.

To find a radio station near you that broadcasts *New Life Live!* go to www.newlife.com.

THE WORRY WORKBOOK

Twelve Steps to Anxiety-Free Living

LEARN HOW TO...

▶ Face your fears and replace them with self-confidence.
▶ Distinguish between what you can and cannot do.
▶ Develop safe relationships that bring out the best in you.
▶ Accept yourself as you are and become an overcomer.

Les Carter, Ph.D. · **Frank Minirth, M.D.**

Authors of the Bestseller *The Anger Workbook*, Over 250,000 Copies in Print

This proven twelve-step program helps individuals understand what causes anxiety and learn how to reduce or eliminate negative stress, anxiety, and frustration.

Worry is one of the most common mood disorders in America. Whether you call it stress, tension, frustration, or anxiety, worry can take its toll on health and well-being. It can be caused by life changes, such as divorce or career upheaval, or it can become a debilitating chronic disorder. *The Worry Workbook* helps readers understand what causes anxiety and how they can move beyond worry into emotional freedom. Practical steps, interactive exercises, checklists, and guided questions help readers identify their fears, replace negative talk with positive action, learn to accept what is out of their control, and make life-enhancing choices. *The Worry Workbook* offers insight on letting go of self-judgment, becoming real, identifying those who help and those who hinder personal growth, and overcoming insecurities—offering those who suffer from anxiety proven ways to find relief.

ISBN: 0-8407-7748-5

MOOD

Understand Your Emotional Highs & Lows
and Achieve a More Balanced & Fulfilled Life

SWINGS

Paul Meier, M.D.
Stephen Arterburn, M.Ed.,
and Frank Minirth, M.D.

Understand Your Emotional Highs and Lows
and Achieve a More Balanced and Fulfilled Life

Seventeen million people in the United States suffer from clinical depression, and more than fifty million people find themselves in prolonged emotional lows. Now, for every sufferer, there is hope. Not only are effective counseling methods available to treat depression, but also researchers have made great strides in understanding the chemical makeup of the brain. *Mood Swings* helps readers understand the causes of "bipolar-related disorders"—and find effective ways to treat the problem, recover the joy they've lost, and return to a far more normal, balanced perspective on life. The doctors discuss the extremes and the in-betweens of depression, and show how the highs and lows of uncontrollable mood swings trap the sufferer in a cycle of dysfunction. *Mood Swings* offers hope to everyone who suffers depression and helps those who love them understand and treat this troubling problem.

ISBN: 0-7852-6771-9

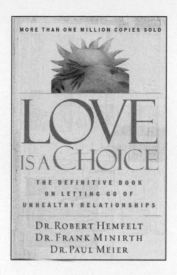

ISBN: 0-7852-7530-4

Dr. Les Carter
Dr. Frank Minirth
THE
ANGER
Workbook

A 13-step interactive plan to help you...
• Understand how unmet needs can feed anger
• Realize how other emotions can influence anger
• Find healthy ways to express and
  control your anger

Don't let anger take control of you!

Most people stereotype anger by assuming that it always results in shout-ing, slamming fists, or throwing things. However, anger is not that one-dimensional. In fact, anger can manifest itself as withdrawal, anxiety, irritability, annoyance, frustration, blowing off steam, and agressiveness. Whether your anger is from tension at work, frustration at home, or just life in general—this workbook will help you identify and modify the anger that keeps you from inner peace and contentment. From doctors nationally recognized in the field of Christian counseling.

ISBN: 0-8407-4574-5